T0155368

GIRLS, INTERRUPTED

Girls,

INTERRUPTED

How Pop Culture
is Failing Women

LISA WHITTINGTON-HILL

Véhicule Press

Published with the generous assistance of the Canada Council for
the Arts and the Canada Book Fund of the Department of
Canadian Heritage.

Cover design by David Drummond
Set in Minion and Gill Sans by Simon Garamond

Copyright © Lisa Whittington-Hill 2023

Dépôt légal, Library and Archives Canada and the
Bibliothèque national du Québec, third trimester 2023

Library and Archives Canada Cataloguing in Publication

Title: Girls, interrupted : how pop culture is failing women /
Lisa Whittington-Hill.
Names: Whittington-Hill, Lisa, author.
Identifiers: Canadiana (print) 20230518478 | Canadiana (EBOOK)
20230518524 | ISBN 9781550656329
(softcover) | ISBN 9781550656404 (EPUB)
Subjects: LCSH: Women in popular culture.
Classification: LCC HQ1233 .W45 2023 | DDC 305.4—dc23

Published by Véhicule Press, Montréal, Québec, Canada
www.vehiculepress.com

Distribution in Canada by LitDistCo
www.litdistco.ca

Distribution in US by Independent Publishers Group
www.ipgbook.com

Printed in Canada

For my Mom
Thank you for always encouraging my love of pop culture
even though it means you've watched more documentaries
about Courtney Love than you ever imagined you would.

xoxo

CONTENTS

Introduction

As a teenager, I traded *Sweet Valley High* books with my friends, watched *Sixteen Candles* until the VHS tape eventually broke, and performed the choreography from Wham's "Wake Me Up Before You Go-Go" video while wearing neon pink fingerless gloves. I read *Teen Beat* and *16*, tearing out pictures of the cast of *The Outsiders* to decorate my locker.

Pop culture consumed me—and still does. I am a proud binge watcher, a proud embracer of celebrity gossip, and a proud lover of oral histories of weird MTV shows you forgot about. Pop culture helps me understand the world around me and make sense of my place in it. It is also a coping mechanism and a source of comfort. When I experience periods of deep depression and anxiety, it has been the thing I curl up with at the end of the day. Never underestimate the healing power of a *Vanderpump Rules* marathon.

But while I'm a fan of pop culture, I've also had a vexed relationship with it. Starting in my pre-teens, it taught me that I was flawed and needed to be fixed. That I must, I must, I must increase my bust. That my hair needed to be blonde and my body thin. If I wanted to date the handsome wrestling team captain (I don't even know if my high school had a wrestling team), I needed someone like Molly Ringwald to give me a makeover during Saturday detention in the library. To this day, I am unable to watch *The Breakfast Club* without wondering where all the materials for that makeover came from. Was there a change of clothes and a hair straightener stashed in a card catalogue? As I got older, pop culture taught me to wake up at 4 a.m. to be productive, that I needed to be married with children to be happy, and that Gwyneth Paltrow's goop could make my life great. Make it stop!

I couldn't make it stop, but I could start to be more skeptical, which eventually led me to arts and culture writing. In the mid-'90s, I enrolled in a two-year journalism program in my hometown of Edmonton, acquired a copy of *The Canadian Press Stylebook,* and dreamed of reviewing *Reality Bites* or analyzing the social messages in Soul Asylum's "Runaway Train" video. This didn't sit well with my classmates, who were very serious about reporting. They wanted to cover politics and break stories about corruption and fraud. But while they were interested in murders, I wanted to write about Murderecords, the east coast record label.

I ended up interning at one of the two alternative weeklies in Edmonton and loved it. My first assignment was to interview Shonen Knife, the all-female Japanese pop-punk band, of which I was a fan. They told me about touring with Nirvana and journalists asking them sexist questions about what it was like to be girls in the music industry. Alternative media outlets were supposed to be progressive, and I had naively believed everyone working with me was too. Despite all the "We're not the mainstream" mantras during weekly staff meetings, I was the only woman working there full time, besides the receptionist. Everyone was white, everyone was cis, everyone was able-bodied, and everyone could afford to be paid in free CDs. It was one of my first experiences with the idea that just calling a space progressive doesn't make it so, and that claiming to question "dominant narratives" doesn't automatically make you more ethical. I would go out for drinks with staff and freelancers and, the more the beer flowed, watch so-called enlightened men behave inappropriately towards women.

One of my favourite hobbies in the '90s was something I affectionately referred to as "arguing at parties with flannel-wearing men about Courtney Love." Men would talk about how Love was crazy, how Kurt Cobain wrote all of her songs, and how she would never have achieved her success without her famous husband. I defended Love, arguing that the media, Nirvana fans, and the music industry mythologized Cobain while vilifying Love—blaming her for everything from his heroin addiction to his suicide. Eventually, my party invites came with a strict "no Courtney clause," which some friends still hold me to.

The Courtney clause, however, helped me see the misogyny she experienced as being widespread. Female musicians keep being accused of not writing their own songs. In 2022, Blur and Gorillaz front man Damon Albarn denied Taylor Swift's abilities as a songwriter, calling her an artist who hides behind "sound and attitude." Swift defended herself. "You don't have to like my songs," she tweeted, "but it's really fucked up to try and discredit my writing." Albarn apologized, saying his comments "had been reduced to clickbait." But everyone knew what he meant. Female stars are consistently underestimated. This attitude is not restricted to songwriting credits either. We are unable to talk about a woman and her art without attaching a man to it. "You will also notice of the big successful female artists, there is always a 'man behind the woman' piece," Lily Allen told *New Musical Express* in 2014. "If it's Beyoncé, it's Jay-Z. If it's Adele, it's Paul Epworth. Me? It was Mark Ronson and the same with Amy Winehouse. You never get that with men."

I also learned that Shonen Knife's complaints were just the tip of the problem. Interviewers couldn't help but ask young female musicians invasive and inappropriate questions. *Meet Me in the Bathroom*, the 2022 documentary that charted the indie music scene that exploded in New York in the early aughts, included clips of interviews with Karen O, lead singer of the band Yeah Yeah Yeahs. She was asked if she had ever had a same-sex experience and if she had received death threats. She remembered photographers aiming their cameras at her crotch. Meanwhile, male bands like The Strokes and Interpol were asked about the best place to listen to their new album or about the process of recording it. Rarely were they asked anything personal.

Sexism extends beyond the media. Este Haim, known for the rock trio Haim, has often called out misogyny and predatory behaviour in the music industry. "I had an experience when we were first getting signed," she told *Teen Vogue* in 2018, describing an encounter with a scout, "and we were doing showcases for labels. After the performance, I was just talking to an A&R, just a normal conversation. Out of nowhere really, he just looks at me and goes, 'So tell me the truth, do you make the same faces on stage that you make in bed?'" Haim have also fought for pay equity in the industry, firing an agent after they found out they were making ten times less than a male artist for a festival appearance. Female musicians also receive mixed messages. "If you speak up for yourself, you're a bitch. If you party too much, you're a whore. Men don't get called these things," Nicki Minaj said in a 2015 interview with *Time*.

The essays in *Girls, Interrupted* explore this double standard. They look at celebrity memoirs, pop culture portrayals of middle-aged women, media coverage of female grifters, and the pressure on pop princesses to constantly reinvent themselves. They describe how the coverage of the mental health and addiction struggles of women like Lindsay Lohan shaped how I talked about my own issues. They explore redemption, and who gets it, as well as unlikeable women and how they get that label. Some pieces are personal, some are the result of hours spent staring at *Us Weekly* covers, some talk about the '90s, some tackle the aughts, and some talk about Jennifer Aniston far more than originally planned. Some are hopeful and offer solutions for how we can do better.

And to be fair, in some ways, we *are* doing better. The past decade has seen a rise in documentaries, memoirs, and podcasts that revisit the legacies of women wronged by pop culture and provide a retelling of their stories and an atonement for our sins. There have been documentaries about Britney Spears and re-examinations of Whitney Houston, Janet Jackson, Pamela Anderson, Sinéad O'Connor, and Brittany Murphy. The sheer number of docuseries and memoirs about female celebrities, as well as women using social media to tell their own stories, reveals not only a demand for this type of story but also just how problematic pop culture's treatment of women has been and how much the pattern has been repeated.

Each day seems to bring fresh examples. As I write this, press coverage of *Spare*, Prince Harry's best-selling memoir, is focused on the supposed feud between Meghan Markle and Kate Middleton (pop culture loves nothing more than two women falling out). On Twitter, trolls are attacking Megan Thee Stallion, unleashing racist and sexist tropes that give the impression she is on trial instead of Tory Lanez, the man eventually found guilty of shooting her. On television, *Fatal Attraction*, the 1987 movie that popularized the "bunny boiler" stereotype of the "vengeful, obsessive, spurned woman," is being rebooted.

I often encounter men who tell me pop culture doesn't have a gender bias problem. Pressed for specifics, they rattle off examples which add up to "Beyoncé" and "ladies winning award things." Movements like #MeToo and #TimesUp, although they have been invaluable, can give the impression that things are now better for women in Hollywood, in publishing, and in the music industry. That the problems have been fixed, that we can pat ourselves on the back for a job well done and move on.

This book exists to prove otherwise.

Lisa Whittington-Hill
Toronto, 2023

The Problem with
Middle-Aged Women

IN THE WEEKS LEADING up to my fiftieth birthday, I avoided my mail. I could feel the tiny metal box taunting me as I tiptoed past it through my apartment lobby. Sometimes I'd open it, peek inside, and then quickly slam the door shut. One of my neighbours caught me and remarked, "It's always bills, right?" But it wasn't my Visa statement that scared me, at least not that month.

Omens of turning a half-century old arrived daily. Medical letters reminding me of all the fun tests I now needed. *Happy Birthday, Lisa. Once you're done celebrating, please don't forget to poop in a box and send it to us!* Bank reminders about the amount I needed to save if I wanted to retire by sixty-five. Promotional offers from a seniors' magazine, aimed at readers aged fifty-five-plus, that promised to help me age gracefully. (My first suggestion would be to not put me in their target readership five years before I need to be.)

I never expected turning fifty would bother me. Other milestone birthdays had passed without a thought—except for eighteen, because I was finally legally able to replace the bottle of Bacardi white rum in the liquor cabinet that my friends and I had been watering down for months (sorry, Mom). I thought a midlife crisis was a myth or, at the very least, a tired cliché. Something that only happened to men, resulting in ill-advised sports car and fedora purchases. I thought I felt comfortable with myself and my life. Like that bottle of watered-down Bacardi, I was clearly faking it.

When I was younger, I equated women over forty-five with Mrs. Roper on *Three's Company*, Mrs. Cunningham on *Happy Days*, or Dorothy on *The Golden Girls*. These roles contributed to a particular idea of who middle-aged women should be, what they should accomplish, and how much space they could take up. I could be a wife or a mom, or I could eat late-night cheesecake in the kitchen with my older lady friends. These were my options, and the cheesecake was the only thing appealing about them.

Thankfully, representations of middle-aged women on screen have since improved. There have been the Housewives both Real and Desperate, Julia Louis-Dreyfus's award-winning turn as Selina Meyer on *Veep*, the ensemble cast of *Big Little Lies*, Pamela Adlon's thinly veiled version of her own life on *Better Things*, and Kate Winslet's flawed cop vaping her way through *Mare of Easttown*. *American Horror Story* has offered great roles for Sarah Paulson, Connie Britton, Angela Bassett, Jessica Lange, and Kathy Bates, and Showtime's *Work in Progress* features comedian Abby McEnany as a self-identifying "fat, queer, dyke" living with both depression and OCD.

These shows have not only increased the visibility of women over a certain age in Hollywood but also provided a range of female characters with more depth than the stereotypical women I saw on television growing up. A 2021 *New York Times* piece argued that Hollywood's ageism problem might finally be dead. That year's Emmys—which saw older women like *Mare of Easttown*'s Winslet (forty-five), *The Crown*'s Gillian Anderson (fifty-three), and Jean Smart of *Hacks* (seventy) take home awards—was just one promising sign. Hollywood's dire gender bias had been perfectly spoofed by comedian Amy Schumer in her 2016 sketch "Last Fuckable Day," which featured Louis-Dreyfus, Tina Fey, and Patricia Arquette mocking the limited opportunities for women over fifty. The facts bear this out: in a 2016 analysis of IMDb data from 1920 to 2011, economists Robert Fleck and Andrew Hanssen found that women in their twenties have a significant advantage over men their age when it comes to leading roles in films, getting 80 percent of them. But as women age, this number decreases, and the gender distribution reverses among actors over forty.

It would seem, then, that things are changing. But ageism operates in more insidious ways. Though representation has improved, pop culture's problem with middle-aged women is far from resolved. They are still wives and moms who are not worthy of their own storylines. Sometimes they are career women, but that also becomes their only identity, and their storyline is focused on how they can't have it all—whatever *all* is. When middle-aged women *are* well represented, it also tends to be a particular type of woman: she is married or divorced and has kids. She is also typically white, heterosexual, cisgender, and thin. All of these trends suggest that middle-agedness still comes with specific, and unfair, expectations for women, and those who don't conform are largely left out of our stories.

And maybe that's part of where my fretting about turning fifty came from. I just wanted the women I saw to move beyond outdated representations of where women "should" be as they age. I wanted pop culture to grow up.

When the birthday I had been dreading for months finally arrived, I actually enjoyed it. I caught up with my family and ate nachos and drank wine with my two closest friends. My dread took the day off, and there was cake! But my anxieties returned two months after my birthday, when Carrie Bradshaw and her Manolos strutted back into my life. HBO Max's *And Just Like That …*, the much-anticipated reboot/sequel to *Sex and the City*, picked up seventeen years after the original show ended.

And Just Like That … was supposed to resonate with me—a fan of the series who was now the same age as the girls. But instead it was an unpleasant reminder of the assumptions our culture has when it comes to middle-aged women. Carrie, Charlotte, and Miranda were now dealing with husbands, children, career transitions, life changes, and Che Diaz's comedy. The show was ramming societal expectations down my throat faster than the girls used to knock back cosmos. I couldn't help but wonder: Was I a failure because my trajectory was different?

Viewers could tell from the first episode that the girls were older. Their reading glasses were thicker (and required) and their lunchtime conversation topics had shifted from modelizers and funky spunk to a discussion about whether Miranda should dye her grey hair to look younger and fit in better with her Columbia classmates. (Her hair was the least of her problems as she managed to alienate most of them with a first class that included misgendering a classmate and racism on a par with that of the second *SATC* movie.) Instead of hitting NYC's hottest clubs, the women now hit children's piano recitals. The show talked about menopause, but only in passing and mostly as a punchline. It also attempted to be more diverse and inclusive than the original series but failed by awkwardly inserting racialized characters who were one dimensional and only existed to prop up the white ladies.

Despite being a show that was largely centred around four unmarried thirtysomethings, *Sex and the City* never had a particularly positive attitude toward single women, often treating them like pathetic pariahs who were just using the Barneys sales as a distraction while they waited to couple up. The new series wasn't much better: it was a painful reminder that older women who have never been married, never had children, or aren't constantly searching for a mate still make pop culture very uncomfortable. As a single woman who has never been married and doesn't have kids, I felt like *And Just Like That . . .* was like that friend who leaves you behind when their life and priorities change. I made it to the end of the season but, more than once, I wanted to turn my television off, write "I'm sorry I can't, don't hate me" on a Post-it Note, slap it on the screen, and head to bed (Jack Berger will always be a legend).

As I kept searching for a faithful depiction of Gen X womanhood, I was surprised to find it in *Yellowjackets*, a show that's, at least on the face of it, about cannibalism and teenagers. In 1996, the Yellowjackets, a women's high school soccer team from New Jersey, are travelling to Seattle for a tournament when their plane crashes somewhere in the Canadian wilderness. The show tells the story of how the girls survived for nineteen months— and, in parallel, it tells the present-day stories of those who escaped from the wild.

The characters on *Yellowjackets* exist in two worlds: as 1996 teenage versions of themselves and as adults now. I found this split-narrative structure relatable. I, too, felt stuck between two worlds. I wanted to cling to the younger version of myself, which *Yellowjackets* reminded me of every week, one Gen X cultural reference and Liz Phair song at a time. But I also had to, painfully, acknowledge the adult version of myself who was getting older and who felt like more than half her life was over. I saw the adult versions of the show's characters, like Melanie Lynskey's Shauna Sadecki, struggling with similar realities.

"Is this really how you thought your life was going to turn out?" That's the question a reporter asks the adult Shauna in one of the show's early episodes as she unpacks groceries in her suburban kitchen. Prior to the plane crash, Shauna was a star athlete and straight-A student, with early acceptance to Brown University and a bright future ahead of her, but now she's a bored, neglected housewife who has strained relationships both with her teenage daughter and her distant husband. Unlike Shauna, I wasn't butchering rabbits in my garden to cope with a midlife crisis, but I was struggling with what gave me purpose and what my life had become. *Yellowjackets* is very good at depicting this tension as characters try to figure out how much they've settled for a life that doesn't resemble what they had imagined when they crashed in the woods as teenagers. These are complicated, messy women—something we usually see only in younger women on shows like *Girls* and *I May Destroy You*.

I had spent much of my younger years, like the high school–aged Yellowjackets, wanting my life to speed up. I couldn't wait to finish high school, to graduate from university, to get my first apartment, my first serious boyfriend, and my first job. Now I wanted the years to take longer to pass. I wasn't in a rush to get to any

23

of the milestones that awaited me in later life. When you're fifty, people say "You have your whole life in front of you" a lot less than they did when you were twenty-five. I thought of Patricia Arquette in the movie *Boyhood* when she says, "You know what's next? It's my fucking funeral! I just thought there would be more."

These days, I think about mortality more than I ever have—mine, my aging mom's, my friends'. Usually, these thoughts occur between the hours of 3 a.m. and 6 a.m., when, in lieu of sleep, I cycle through my life's regrets or look up junior high bullies on LinkedIn—the volleyball-mean-girl-to-health-and-wellness-blogger pipeline is very much alive and well in my hometown. I think of what-ifs and "what could have been" and how pixie cuts never worked with my face shape. I've always been an introvert who enjoyed a lot of time alone, but now my independence, once a source of pride, resembles something closer to loneliness.

Yellowjackets highlights two groups pop culture has often struggled with when it comes to representation—teenage girls and middle-aged women—and places both at the centre of the story. This helped me acknowledge the parts of my younger self that still existed: both the ones I was willing to let go of and those I still wanted to embrace. It also helped middle-age me feel less invisible in a world that I increasingly felt was trying to erase me.

When actor Keanu Reeves went public with his relation-ship with artist Alexandra Grant, tabloids and celebrity-gossip sites repeatedly commented on Grant's natural grey hair and her "age appropriateness" (she's forty-nine, compared to Reeves's fifty-seven), which is Hollywood code for "old." The internet also incorrectly identified her as Helen Mirren, because if you have grey hair and are over a certain age in Hollywood, there's only one option for you: Helen Mirren. When tabloids and the internet aren't mixing up their greys, they're telling women they look too old and then shaming them when they have work done that makes them look younger.

I am constantly reminded of how my body has changed: the lines on my face, the grey in my hair, the weight I have gained. None of my clothes fit anymore, so for what felt like weeks on end, I wore bright-red jogging pants from the Gap and a "Free Winona" (as in Ryder) T-shirt that had always been too big but now felt uncomfortably snug. On my way to work one day, I ran into a friend who eyed my outfit and then asked if I was coming from the gym. If you know me, you know I am unlikely to ever be coming from the gym, and if I am, it will be the first thing I mention because I will expect a parade or commemorative plaque.

I increasingly feel self-conscious about dressing in an age-appropriate way. In an episode of *Hacks*, aging comedian Deborah Vance describes all the effects menopause and aging have on a woman's body, from grey hair to cracked nails, before calling it "Mother Nature's way of telling you to get to the back of the cave." I know I will eventually have to retire my red track pants.

Until then, I have purchased them in four more colours. Searching for a replacement, I spent far too much time reading online reviews of clothing before putting the items in my cart to make sure the dresses I wanted hit below the knee.

It's been two years since my fiftieth birthday. In that time, I have become more hopeful about representations of aging women in pop culture. I see more Gen X women on television and more opportunities for actresses. Even middle-aged Carrie Bradshaw is a more developed character than Mrs. Roper or Mrs. Cunningham.

I've tried to adapt to my ongoing midlife crisis. I didn't buy a sports car, but I did spend far too much money on vintage 1990s concert tees online. My advances toward younger men have been restricted to defending Pete Davidson in work Zoom meetings. I try to worry less about death and how much time I have left. My friends and I half-heartedly joke about whose parents have accumulated the most clutter in their homes and who will have a bigger mess on their hands when they have to downsize Mom or Dad or both. When I visited my mom's house in my twenties, I used to try to sneak in after a night out without waking her. Now when I visit, I try to sneak out without her stuffing Lady Diana commemorative thimbles or pieces of her china into my suitcase.

I need all the room I can get for my track pants.

Judge a Book Not
by its Gender

I BLAME DREW BARRYMORE for two things: a botched attempt to dye my hair the same platinum blonde as her locks in a 1993 Guess Jeans ad and the small fortune I've dropped on celebrity memoirs.

Little Girl Lost, Barrymore's 1990 account of growing up as a child star in Hollywood, ignited my love of show-business tell-alls, especially by women. My dog-eared copy has survived book purges and cross-country moves. It's an appreciation others shared. The coming-of-age tale was a *New York Times* bestseller and, although now out of print, has achieved cult-like status. It was even the subject of a 2018 *New York Times Magazine* Letter of Recommendation.

Barrymore was just eleven months old when she got her start in a Puppy Chow television commercial. At seven, she starred as Gertie in Steven Spielberg's blockbuster 1982 film *E.T.* and that same year became the youngest person to ever host *Saturday Night Live*. Barrymore's drug and alcohol use began shortly after *E.T.* phoned home. The first time she got drunk, she was nine. She started smoking weed at ten and by twelve had moved on to cocaine. The actress entered rehab at thirteen, and during her second stint in rehab, she completed *Little Girl Lost*, which was published when she was sixteen.

Juicy stories about nightclubbing with Jack Nicholson definitely make for a good read, but what initially drew me to the book was that Barrymore wrote it to counter stories about herself in the *National Enquirer*. "[I]magining the godawful headlines—'Drew Barrymore Cocaine Addict at Twelve Years Old' or 'Barrymore Burns Out in Teens'—and the impression people would get of me was all my worst possible fears come true. I would've been the last person on Earth to deny my problems, but I wanted to have the option of confessing them," Barrymore writes in *Little Girl Lost*. She wanted to come clean about her past on her own terms, a desire that not only compelled me to read her book but has made me return to it over the years.

Redirecting one's life story is a major reason celebrities embrace the memoir genre, but it is not the only reason. Some stars do it to revive a stalled career. For others, memoirs extend their fifteen minutes of fame. This is a popular motivation for reality show stars. (Will you accept this rose and this six-figure book deal?) Memoirs also settle old scores. In André Leon Talley's *The Chiffon Trenches: A Memoir*, the fashion journalist and former *Vogue* creative director works through his issues with *Vogue* editor Anna Wintour. Memoirs can also promote the brand a star has built around themselves. Reese Witherspoon's *Whiskey in a Teacup*, which markets the star's Southern Lifestyle to y'all, or any book from one of *Queer Eye*'s Fab Five are great examples.

For readers, celebrity memoir appeal lies in the industry gossip and name dropping and the chance to peek inside the glamorous lifestyles of the rich and famous. Social media, reality television, celebrity blogs, and *TMZ*-style tabloid journalism have created an insatiable desire to know more about our favourite celebrities. Memoirs help meet that demand. Sometimes, unfortunately, we learn a little too much. After reading Carrie Fisher's *The Princess Diarist*, her third memoir, I can't watch *Star Wars* without thinking about all the coke Fisher said was consumed on set. I imagine the film's stars hollowing out lightsabers to use like giant straws to blow rails with. (That's not how the force works!)

It's easy to dismiss celebrity memoirs as fluff, but you cannot deny the genre's popularity. One of the best-selling celebrity memoirs of all time, former first lady Michelle Obama's 2018 *Becoming*, has sold more than 10 million copies. If celebrity memoirs have become big business, we have Rolling Stones co-founder and guitarist Keith Richards to thank. *Life*, for which Richards received a $7 million advance, was published in 2010 and sold over 1 million copies in its first year. So successful was Richards's book that more celebrity autobiographies were published in the four years that followed than in the previous fifteen, and these included books by male musicians from Duff McKagan to Steven Tyler (both bestsellers).

Of course, it's not just men penning hits. Since first reading *Little Girl Lost* at twenty, I have devoured memoirs by female celebrities, from punk singer Alice Bag's *Violence Girl: East LA Rage to Hollywood Stage, a Chicana Punk Story* to *Jersey Shore* star Snooki's *Confessions of a Guidette*. Remember how, after *Bossypants* came out, we all decided women were funny? Tina Fey's 2011 best-selling memoir preceded an onslaught of books by funny ladies, including Mindy Kaling's *Is Everyone Hanging Out Without Me? (And Other Concerns)* and Amy Poehler's *Yes Please*.

But it didn't take long for me to realize that, when compared to what men were writing, memoirs by celebrity women were a different artifact altogether. There's a contrast in how they are marketed, the topics they are expected to cover, and how much of themselves the stars are expected to expose. The gender divide becomes more problematic, and downright depressing, when you watch how the memoirs are greeted by critics. Rather than assessing a given book on its own terms, reviewers revert to stereotypes and clichés. In the process, they miss the actual story. Women can spend chapters on their awards, accolades, and accomplishments. Reviewers still focus only on sex, scandal, and bombshell reveals. When it comes to celebrity memoirs written by women, sadly, we haven't come a long way, baby.

Debbie Harry's 2019 *Face It* had been highly anticipated. In the memoir, the punk icon chronicles everything from her adoption at three months and her days in the all-girl group The Stilettos to forming both Blondie the band and Blondie the persona. For Harry, Blondie was very much a character she played, one inspired by the "Hey, blondie!" catcalls she received from construction workers after bleaching her hair as well as the 1930s *Blondie* comic strip character. Marilyn Monroe was also a muse; Harry describes Monroe as "the proverbial dumb blonde with the little-girl voice and big-girl body" who, despite her appearance, has "a lot of smarts behind the act."

Face It also covers Harry's acting in films like *Videodrome* and *Hairspray*, her time training as a professional wrestler for a role in the Broadway play *Teaneck Tanzi: The Venus Flytrap* as well as her activism and philanthropy work. (Fun fact: she was almost Pris in *Blade Runner*, but her record company made her turn it down.) There is certainly no shortage of great material for reviewers to discuss. Unfortunately, they responded with sexist tropes.

"In her memoir, Debbie Harry proves she's more than just a pretty blonde in tight pants," read the headline in the *Washington Post*. It was later changed to "In her memoir, Debbie Harry gives an unvarnished look at her life in the punk scene" after social media backlash. But the headline was not the review's only problem.

Here's how it opens: "Even if Debbie Harry, of the band Blondie, isn't to your taste—her voice too thin, her sexiness too blatant, her music too smooth—you can't dismiss certain truths about her." The disdain drips from every word. I read Bruce Springsteen's 2016 memoir *Born to Run* at the same time as *Face It*. How did the *Post* begin its review of the Boss? "Why, one might ask, would Bruce Springsteen need to write an autobiography? Haven't we been listening to it for the past half century? Hasn't he been telling us his story all along?" He has shared so much through his music; what more could he possibly give us? (You can sit this one out, Bruce. I have heard *Atlantic City* and do not require any further emoting from you at this time.)

The *Post* review of *Face It* goes from bad to worse. When it isn't criticizing Harry for being "self-interested" (I did not see any complaints about Springsteen's seventy-nine chapters), it ogles the sensational aspects of her story. "She had a hookup with an Andy Warhol protégé in a phone booth in Max's Kansas City," runs one typical sentence, "and began what she blithely calls 'chipping and dipping' in heroin." There's no better lesson in the realities of being a female musician than to have a lifetime of trailblazing reduced to your sex life and drug use.

Control is a central theme of *Face It*, whether that control is extended to her image, her band, or her art. Early in the book, Harry recounts a record company promoting Blondie's first album with posters of her in a see-through blouse despite early assurances that the posters would feature only headshots and would include all band members. She was not happy with the marketing decision, saying, "Sex sells, that's what they

32

say, and I'm not stupid, I know that. But on my terms, not some executive's."

And while doing things on her own terms is a source of pride for Harry, reviewers seem to have a serious problem with it. "[W]hat's a memoir for, if not to pull back the curtain and check out the lady who is pushing the buttons?" asks Harry in *Face It*. But when the curtain doesn't pull back as much as the reviewers want, they become resentful, sullen, and offended. *The Atlantic*'s review reads almost like it begrudges Harry the permission to tell her story on her own terms— "holding back," it says, "is an understandable maneuver for someone who's been stared at so much."

The *Guardian* was also annoyed that Harry did not give away enough of herself. "It's a shame that Harry passes up the chance to dig deeper into her experiences of objectification and the nature of fame, but more disappointing is that we learn so little about her interior life, and how she really thinks and feels." I guess talking about being raped at knifepoint is not enough. What's with the heart of glass, Debbie? Give us more of your pain! And on page five, not 105!

The headline of *Rolling Stone*'s review highlights how Harry's book "looks back on what she learned from Andy Warhol and David Bowie." It's as if the only way we can understand art by women is in the context of the men who orbit around them. Despite writing 368 pages about herself, the only interesting thing about Harry— according to *Rolling Stone*—is the famous male company she kept.

The *New York Times* was no better. Its review manages to make it all the way to the fourth paragraph before it mentions her age. It also talks about the number of memoirs by female rockers being released at the same time as Harry's book. ("[T]here's a bit of a pileup of female rockers getting reflective this season.") It fixates on the fact that Harry's "face is unlined" and focuses on her "crisp red collared blouse with white polka dots and red leggings."

Two weeks after *Face It* came out, another musical icon released a memoir. *Me* by Elton John covers the singer's childhood in the London suburb of Pinner and his early musical days in Los Angeles. He also writes about his songwriting partnership with Bernie Taupin, his successful solo career, his cocaine addiction, and his marriage and family with husband David Furnish. Keen readers might be quick to point out that his title is the same as that of actress Katharine Hepburn's memoir. Is there anything men will not just unapologetically lay claim to?

While *Rolling Stone*'s review name-checked Harry's famous male friends in its headline, they didn't bother to do that with John's book. "Elton John's *Me* Is A Uniquely Revealing Pop Star Autobiography," runs the banner. The review concedes the book as "skimpy on revelations about his brilliant, ground breaking music" but calls it "essential reading" anyway.

Entertainment Weekly's description of *Me* is also glowing: "While *Me* is as colourful as you'd expect from an artist famous for his outlandish stage costumes and outsize temper tantrums, it is also so much more than

34

simply a dishy sex, drugs, and rock 'n roll tell-all." Did you catch that? The memoir may have sex and drugs, but those scandalous elements shouldn't be used to sum up a career. At least, it shouldn't if you're a male celebrity.

Can you feel the love tonight? Not yet? Never fear, here comes the *Guardian*. Its review opens with, "[C]hoosing one's favourite Elton song—can feel like limiting oneself to a mere single grape from the horn of plenty." The *Daily Mail* calls it "the rock memoir of the decade," while for the *Washington Post*, it is an "unsparing, extravagantly funny new memoir" and "bracingly honest."

It's hard to find criticism about *Me*, yet the book is far from perfect. It abounds in stories about legendary friends like Stevie Wonder, Yoko Ono, John Lennon, Andy Warhol, and Neil Young, yet the anecdotes leave readers feeling like they never get to peek behind the shiny veneer of John's fame. Then there's all the insensitive writing. "You think you're being difficult, my little sausage? Have I ever told you about the time I drank eight vodka martinis, took all my clothes off in front of a film crew, and then broke my manager's nose?" he writes, comparing his bad behaviour to, of all things, his son's tantrums. Harry, at least, is more self-aware and deconstructs the misconceptions and preconceptions that fans, the media, and other musicians have of her.

But John doesn't have to worry about owning up to his behaviour. No one seems to care. For all their talk of his addiction to cocaine, the reviews are quick to follow up with redemption stories: "While his extraordinary talent justified his personal excesses, it is his self-awareness that has counterbalanced the narcissism and made him such a likable figure."

If we examine the media's reaction to female celebrity memoirs, it becomes painfully clear that this redemption narrative is strictly reserved for the boys.

Actress, producer, and director Demi Moore's memoir, *Inside Out*, was released a few weeks before John's, and the tabloids had a feeding frenzy. Like John, Moore struggled with addiction. Unlike John, journalists never let her forget it—along with other parts of her story.

"Demi Moore drops shocking revelations about Ashton Kutcher, sexual assault and sobriety," reads the headline in the *LA Times*. The story proceeds to break down Moore's childhood pain, her miscarriage, Ashton Kutcher cheating on her, and her struggles with alcohol and drugs.

More than one review talks about how Bruce Willis and Kutcher must feel about Demi airing their dirty laundry. As with Debbie Harry, it seems we cannot talk about Moore without mentioning the famous men in her life. Was Bruce mad? What does Ashton really think?

Entertainment Weekly's piece ran with the headline "Celebrities react to Demi Moore's revealing memoir *Inside Out*." Unsurprisingly, all the celebrities quoted in the piece were men. (Also, if one more reviewer mentions how great Moore looks for her age, I will make them watch—on repeat, until they beg for mercy—that awful scene in *St. Elmo's Fire* where Rob Lowe's character passionately details the origin story of St. Elmo's Fire while performing pyrotechnics with a can of aerosol hairspray and a lighter.)

Most of Moore's memoir coverage focused on its tabloid aspects. Read the headlines to see if you can spot a trend:

"7 Biggest Bombshells From Demi Moore's Explosive Memoir" (*accessonline.com*)

"Demi Moore: 8 Biggest Bombshells From Her Memoir *Inside Out*" (*popculture.com*; also, take that, *accessonline.com*)

"Demi Moore's raw *Inside Out* reveals rape, why marriage to Ashton Kutcher crumbled" (*USA Today*)

"Demi Moore Gets Real About Her Painful Childhood, Drugs, Ashton Kutcher, and Other Exes in New Book *Inside Out*" (Stay classy, *Us Weekly*)

"Demi Moore drops shocking revelations about Ashton Kutcher, sexual assault and sobriety" (*LA Times*)

"Why Demi Moore Fulfilled Ashton Kutcher's Threesome Fantasies" (*E! Online*)

The unfortunate thing about these headlines is that, as with Harry, Moore's candour is used to undermine her real achievements. Moore got her acting start in 1981 as Jackie Templeton on *General Hospital*, the number one show on daytime television at the time. She followed that up with roles in films like the Brat Pack bonanzas *St. Elmo's Fire* and *About Last Night.*

Then she got what many, including Moore, consider to be a turning point in her career. "This could be an absolute disaster, or it could be amazing," she writes of reading the script for *Ghost*, which ended up being a big hit in 1990, grossing over $500 million. It was nominated for five Oscars and four Golden Globes, including a Golden Globes best actress nomination for Moore.

Moore followed the success of *Ghost* with *A Few Good Men*, *Indecent Proposal*, and *Striptease*, a film for which she was offered over $12 million, an amount that, at the time, made her the highest paid actress in Hollywood. "But instead of people seeing my big payday as a step in the right direction for women or calling me an inspiration," she writes in her memoir, "they came up with something else to call me: Gimmie Moore." It is worth noting that, at the time, her husband Bruce Willis had just been paid $20 million for the third *Die Hard* movie. (Yippee-Ki-Yay indeed!)

"She became a movie star in this time where women didn't naturally fit into the system," said Gwyneth Paltrow, a friend of Moore's, in the *New York Times* piece on *Inside Out*. "She was really the first person who fought for pay equality and got it, and really suffered a backlash from it. We all certainly benefited from her."

And while it pains me greatly to side with someone who talks about vagina steaming, Paltrow's right. Moore is an inspiration, and fighting for equal pay in Hollywood should be one of the things the media focuses on when they talk about *Inside Out*. Sadly, it is not. Ashton Kutcher and threesomes get the upper hand over the many empowering parts of her life.

Remember her iconic *Vanity Fair* cover? Shot in 1991 by Annie Leibovitz when Moore was seven months pregnant with her second daughter, Scout, it's considered one of the most influential magazine covers of all time. Legendary former *Esquire* art director George Lois described it as a "brave image on the cover of a great magazine—a stunning work of art that conveyed a potent message that challenged a repressed society." Let's talk about that!

Or her intense training for her role in *G.I. Jane*, a 1997 film she both starred in and produced. "I was emotionally invested in the story, the message and the provocative questions it raised," she says of the film. The film was panned by critics, and Moore talks at length in *Inside Out* about her disappointment at the reception to a project that meant so much to her.

The sections where Moore talks about Hollywood's double standards, whether it be the pay gap or reactions to the age difference between her and Kutcher, are some of the best parts of the book. Unfortunately, they are the parts covered least.

The last line of *Inside Out* is: "But we all suffer, and we all triumph, and we all get to choose how we hold both." It is a great line, but in Moore's case, while she may get to choose how she holds both, the media will only ever be interested in her suffering.

Jessica Simpson released her memoir, *Open Book*, in February 2020. It reached number one on the *New York Times* Best Seller list, but like Moore's, Simpson's book promptly became tabloid fodder. "Jessica's Shocking Confessions," reads the *Star* headline on a piece that focuses on Simpson's struggles with drug and alcohol abuse and her famous exes. Like Moore, Simpson is now sober.

Simpson was signed to Columbia Records in 1997 at seventeen. The label's answer to Britney Spears and Christina Aguilera, she went on to release six best-selling records. She also starred in the MTV reality show *Newlyweds: Nick and Jessica*, which featured Simpson and then husband and 98 Degrees singer Nick Lachey, who, at the time, was the more successful of the two. If you don't remember Lachey from MTV, you might know him from his gig hosting Netflix's *Love Is Blind*.

Newlyweds, a ratings success, aired for two years. While it made the couple into household names, it was Simpson who stole the show with her ditzy, dumb blonde antics. Her confusion over whether Chicken of the Sea was chicken or tuna earned her a place in both reality television and pop culture history. The most interesting parts of *Open Book* are when Simpson talks about her reality television persona and the identity crisis it led to. "How was I supposed to live a real healthy life filtered through the lens of a reality show? If my personal life was my work, and my work required me to play a certain role, who even was I anymore?" she writes.

Open Book is Simpson's attempt to distance herself from her *Newlyweds* role and change perceptions of her, a common reason people write memoirs. Some get it—"You Remember Jessica Simpson, Right? Wrong," reads the headline on the *New York Times* piece about her memoir—but, unfortunately, most reviewers don't. Simpson has moved beyond her *Newlyweds* character. She's built a billion-dollar fashion and licensing business and is a mom to three kids, but the media seems indifferent to her new roles, preferring to keep her forever stuck in 2003, in her UGG boots and pink Juicy Couture tracksuit, confused about tuna.

Simpson talks about the effect this identity crisis had on her. She also discusses her sexual abuse at the age of six, her struggles with weight and body image, as well as her addiction to alcohol and pills. She started to increasingly rely on alcohol during her relationship with singer John Mayer in 2006, insecure that she wasn't smart enough to date him. My heart breaks when I think of Simpson wasting time worrying about being the intellectual equal of the man who gave us the musical profundity that is "Your Body Is a Wonderland" and later referred to sex with Simpson as "sexual napalm."

But what troubles me most is how, after learning about how Mayer brought out her insecurities, the media thought it was a good idea to focus on his reaction to *Open Book*. I know this guy was always judging you, Jessica, so we thought it might be fun to ask him what he thought of your book!

Celebs don't always take artistic licence with the story-telling form, but when they do, the gender divide is strictly enforced. Singer and songwriter Liz Phair's *Horror Stories* isn't a straightforward, linear autobiography so much as an unconventional collection of essays.

Through tales about blizzards, blackouts (from lack of electricity, not drinking), marital infidelity, giving birth to her son, and getting dressed up to go to Trader Joe's, Phair reveals a lot about herself and about identity, insecurity, fame, and regret. "In the stories that make up this book, I am trusting you with my deepest self," she writes in the book's prologue. Turns out Phair's deepest self was too hard to find for those fuck-and-run readers who were too busy complaining about her non-traditional style.

Many of the complaints centred on the fact that *Horror Stories* barely mentions Phair's music, including, and especially, her influential 1993 album *Exile in Guy-ville*. A song-by-song reply to the 1972 Rolling Stones album *Exile on Main St.*, it was the number one album on year-end lists from *Spin* and the *Village Voice* and was rated the fifth best album of the 1990s by *Pitchfork*.

"[A] landmark of foul-mouthed, comprised intimacy, a tortured confessional, a workout in female braggadocio, and a wellspring of penetrating self-analysis and audacity" is how *The New Yorker* celebrated the twentieth anniversary of *Exile in Guyville*'s release.

Horror Stories didn't bring it up. "Phair's new memoir *Horror Stories* makes little mention of the album or her artistic life," reads the *Washington Post*'s review; "the absence of concrete stories about *Exile in Guyville* is palpable," writes *Pitchfork*. "Her relationship to music seems to have been the longest and maybe the most demanding love of her life, the one for which she has been willing to get lost, to fail, and to try again over and over for decades. Call me a selfish fan, but I have to say that is one story in all its horror and passion I would love to hear," reads the review in the *New York Times*.

Remember how the *Post* thought that Springsteen did not need to write his memoir, *Born to Run*, because he had revealed so much in his songs already? Why didn't Phair get the same consideration? Reviewers focused so much on what was missing that they missed what was there. Well, maybe not *all* of what was there. In chapter 14 of *Horror Stories*, called "Hashtag," Phair writes about waking up one morning to headlines about the rock star who was supposed to produce her next album. The *New York Times* broke the story about multiple women, including his ex-wife Mandy Moore, coming forward to accuse Ryan Adams of manipulative behaviour, sexual misconduct, emotional and verbal abuse, and harassment. The FBI was also investigating him for sexually explicit exchanges with an underage fan.

In the chapter, Phair talks about her own experiences with sexual assault, sexual harassment, stalkers, and the sexism she experienced in the music industry. She writes about being instructed by a record label president to let radio programmers "feel her up a little" because it would help boost her career, or about being told that she would never work again if she didn't go along with sexy photo shoots. But the press passed over these stories.

Instead, Phair was frequently asked about Adams and her experience working with him. "I don't want every headline about this book that is so important to me to be about Ryan Adams," she tells *Entertainment Weekly*. She is annoyed when a male reporter from *New York Magazine* returns again and again to Adams, including his process as a producer. (Because when I hear about a man accused of sexual misconduct, the first thing I wonder about is his artistic process.) "Out of everything in the book, why is the Ryan Adams thing such an interesting topic?" Phair asks him. "It does need to be talked about, but so do the larger issues."

There are celebrities who aren't judged by the unusual ways they tell their story. Celebrities who, if they go off script, or resist giving readers what they want or expect, aren't rejected by reviewers. Of course, those celebrities are typically men.

Acid for the Children, the 2019 memoir by Red Hot Chili Peppers bassist Flea (aka Michael Balzary), explores Flea's childhood growing up in Australia, his relationship with his older sister, Karyn, his family's move to the US when he was four, his first crush, how Kurt Vonnegut Jr. changed his life, and his love of basketball and the Sony Walkman. He talks about meeting Red Hot Chili Peppers lead singer, Anthony Kiedis, in 1976 at Fairfax High School, about learning to play bass, about his first band, Anthym, about shooting coke and taking speed, his time in the California punk band Fear, and about acting in the 1983 movie *Suburbia*. There are also lists of the concerts that changed his life, books that blew his mind, and movies that grew him.

Lots of great material, right? You know what's missing? Anything about the Red Hot Chili Peppers, the best-selling, Grammy-winning, Rock-and-Roll-Hall-of-Fame-inducted band he founded, plays bass in, and is most strongly associated with.

Flea's book ends just as Tony Flow and the Miraculously Majestic Masters of Mayhem, what would later become the Red Hot Chili Peppers, play their first show at the Grandia Room in Los Angeles to twenty-seven people in February 1983. This performance comes up on page 375 of the 385-page book. There's no mention of the Red Hot Chili Peppers, his movie roles beyond *Suburbia* (*My Own Private Idaho* being one of his most famous), his role as a father of two girls, how he founded the Silverlake Conservatory of Music, or his work with other musicians, from Thom Yorke's Atoms for Peace to Alanis Morissette. (Flea played bass on "You Oughta Know," her hit single from 1995's *Jagged Little Pill*.)

The book is about Flea's journey *to* the band, rather than *with* it. Surely, reviewers were as outraged by this omission as they were when Phair failed to talk about *Exile in Guyville*? Will it surprise you to know they were not fussed at all? Rather than complain about what was missing from *Acid for the Children*, the coverage assessed what was there and praised Flea for it. "[H]e's actually a lovely writer, with a particular gift for the free-floating and reverberant," reads the review in *The Atlantic*. "He writes in Beat Generation bursts and epiphanies, lifting toward the kind of virtuosic vulnerability and self-exposure associated with the great jazz players." If you want to dream of Californication, in other words, you will have to do it somewhere else.

To be clear: this is a good thing. Reviewers *should* be able to see, and appreciate, Flea as something other than just the bassist for the Red Hot Chili Peppers. The problem is that a very different set of rules applies to a female celebrity. The more tell-all her memoir, the more trauma-ridden, the better. She must bare it all, page after page. Men like Flea can operate by a different playbook. They can leave out the scar tissue. Female celebrities like Debbie and Demi are never just human beings writing about their lives. Reviewers are unable to abandon their preconceived notions, their ideas of who these women are, their celebrity personas and just see them as people who should be allowed to tell stories their way.

In an interview with *Entertainment Weekly*, Flea said that his goal with *Acid for the Children* was that "it could be a book that could live beyond being a celebrity book or a rock star book and just stand on its own as a piece of literature." I can only imagine the outrage if Debbie Harry wrote *Face It* and the book ended with, "And then I started this band Blondie. See you later!" Or if Demi Moore ended *Inside Out* with, "Then I got the part in this movie *St. Elmo's Fire*. The end." Or if Courtney Love wrote her memoir (please do this, Courtney) and the last page read, "And then I met this guy Kurt, but I have to go be the girl with the most cake now. Peace out." The fact that Love and her accomplishments are forever tied to her husband is a whole other gender bias problem.

Of course, Flea is not the first Red Hot Chili Pepper to give it away in a celebrity memoir. In 2004, Kiedis published *Scar Tissue*, his *New York Times* bestseller about his life in the band and his time in and out of rehab, as well as in and out of various women. If you have ever thought, "I bet Anthony Kiedis does well with the ladies but would really like to get a better sense of his success rate," then this is the book for you. In his memoir, Kiedis dishes out debauchery, depravity, and drug abuse in a way that reads like a *Behind the Music* episode on steroids. (See any book by a current or past member of Mötley Crüe or Guns N' Roses for a further look at this style.) A woman would never get away with writing about drugs like Kiedis does.

The price for female celebrities who write about addiction is that they have to sound self-aware and apologetic. The mandatory tone is: "I know I am a drug addict, and I keep messing up, but I'm really sorry, and please stick with me 'cause I am gonna sort this out." For great examples of this, see *How to Murder Your Life* by fashion and beauty journalist Cat Marnell and *More, Now, Again: A Memoir of Addiction* from *Prozac Nation* author Elizabeth Wurtzel, who passed away in 2020. Also, I would like to point out the blurbs on the backs of *Scar Tissue* by Kiedis and *How to Murder Your Life* by Marnell in case you still doubt there's a gender bias when it comes to how celebrity memoirs are received.

"Hot Bukowski," -*Rolling Stone* on Marnell.

"A frank, unsparing, meticulous account of a life lived entirely on impulse, for pleasure, and for kicks," -*Time* on Kiedis.

(Oh, and if you are reading this and you're in charge of greenlighting Red Hot Chili Peppers memoirs, can you please get guitarist John Frusciante working on his? Frusciante is known for talking at length both about his connection to spirits—he might already have a ghostwriter!—and about different dimensions and worlds. If there is a book by a band member to be written, this is the one.)

It is impossible to talk about Flea's book without also mentioning the title, *Acid for the Children*, which comes from a song by a band called Too Free Stooges. How far do you think Moore would have gotten if she had called her memoir *Whippets for the Wee Ones*? Instead, memoir titles by women follow a specific pattern: *Hunger Makes Me a Modern Girl*, by Sleater-Kinney's Carrie Brownstein, *The Girl in the Back* by 1970s drummer Laura Davis-Chanin, *Girl in a Band* by Sonic Youth's Kim Gordon, and *Not That Kind of Girl* by actress and *Girls* creator Lena Dunham.

All the titles mention "girl" as if there is a need to announce that early on and get it out of the way. Compare these with the dude titles. There's *Life* by Keith Richards, *Slash* by Slash, *The Heroin Diaries* by Nikki Sixx, and *In the Pleasure Groove* by John Taylor.

I do not know what the pleasure groove is, but I do hope it is also the name of the kickass yacht in Duran Duran's "Rio" video.

Acid for the Children is not the only recent celebrity memoir by a man to resist the traditional memoir style and receive zero criticism for it. It's a courtesy extended to them even after their death. Singer and songwriter Prince's *The Beautiful Ones*, named for the song from *Purple Rain*, lacked the typical style of a life story.

"He wanted to write the biggest music book in the world, one that would serve as a how-to-guide for creatives, a primer on African American entrepreneurship and a 'handbook for the brilliant community,'" wrote Dan Piepenbring, an editor at *The Paris Review*, who was working on the book with Prince. Notoriously private, to the point that reporters were not allowed to record their interviews with the singer, Prince surprised many with his decision to write his life story at all. He wanted his book contract to state he could pull it from shelves if he felt the work no longer reflected him, which just seems like a very Prince thing to do.

The twist is that its subject died just one month after the book's publication was announced. Prince had completed just thirty handwritten pages before he died of an accidental fentanyl overdose on April 21, 2016. The pages detailed his childhood and his early days as a musician. Piepenbring returned to Prince's Paisley Park compound months after the singer's death to find additional material that could be used in the book. This material includes personal photos, drawings, song lyrics, and a handwritten synopsis of *Purple Rain*, Prince's 1984 film that marked his acting debut. The addition of personal artifacts to round out the story means *The Beautiful Ones* is more scrapbook than memoir. "*The Beautiful Ones* does not offer a clear-eyed view of who Prince really was—he would have hated that, but it illuminates more than it conceals," wrote the *Washington Post*.

Reading reviews of *The Beautiful Ones*, I wondered what would have happened if Prince were a woman? Would they have focused on the singer's drug use, final days, and death?

Prince's life ended in respect and a beautiful tribute in book form—and glowing reviews for it. This respect is definitely missing when we pay tribute to female celebrities who have died. Their deaths provide another opportunity for the media to pick them apart and let their scandals overshadow their contributions. I'm thinking here of "The Devils in the Diva," the gossip-heavy *Vanity Fair* piece from 2012 on the late singer and actress Whitney Houston, which "investigates Houston's final days: the prayers and the parties, the Hollywood con artist on the scene, and the message she left behind." Or the less-than-respectful movies made about female celebrities after their deaths that focus more on their personal lives and troubles than they do on their art. Even in death, women like Houston are still expected to bare all.

Girls Gone Grift

FROM 2013 TO 2017, German heiress Anna Delvey ran up huge unpaid bills at fancy New York City hotels, swindled banks out of tens of thousands of dollars, forged financial documents using Microsoft Word, and conned her way onto a private jet. When she was arrested in 2017, Delvey turned out to be a phoney. Her real name was Anna Sorokin, and she was born to a working-class family in Russia. Her trial, which ended in May 2019—her charges included attempted grand larceny, grand larceny in the second degree, and theft of services—obsessed me. I wasn't alone.

New York's 2018 story about Delvey, one of the magazine's most-read pieces that year, was turned into a Shonda Rhimes–produced Netflix series called *Inventing Anna*. When it premiered in February 2022, it was, at the time, the most-watched English-language series in a one-week period, with 196 million hours of viewing time. Delvey was also the subject of a 2018 *Vanity Fair* piece by Rachel DeLoache Williams, who later accused Sorokin of cheating her out of $62,000 while the two were on a trip to Marrakesh (Delvey was found not guilty). Williams's book, *My Friend Anna: The True Story of a Fake Heiress*, was, at one point, optioned for television by actor and producer Lena Dunham. Delvey's story has also been featured in podcasts, documentary shows, and even turned into a stage play.

Pop culture has a long history with male scammers, from Leonardo DiCaprio's portrayal of Frank Abagnale in *Catch Me If You Can* to fraudsters like Bernie Madoff and Simon Leviev, who used Tinder to swindle women out of tens of thousands of dollars. But women are getting in on the game too. In addition to Delvey, there was Elizabeth Holmes, founder and CEO of the now-defunct health technology company Theranos, which promised to revolutionize blood testing. There was also Sarma Melngailis, star of the Netflix documentary *Bad Vegan*, who helped her ex-husband steal millions from employees and investors. Women are not only the subjects of these stories, they're also the target audience. Statistics show that true crime is increasingly consumed by females.

In her 2021 book *Confident Women: Swindlers, Grifters, and Shapeshifters of the Female Persuasion*, Tori Telfer suggested that the appeal of the female con artist lies in jealousy. "Most people, especially women, live their lives rattling around inside a thousand and one social barriers," she wrote. "But, through some mysterious alchemy of talent and criminality, the con artist bursts through those barriers like Houdini escaping from one of his famous suspended straitjackets." For Telfer, these women embody a selfishness viewers find not only shocking but "delicious."

This explains our obsession with fictional female grifters, from the duping dames in movies like *Ocean's 8* and *Hustlers* to Rosamund Pike's turn as a court-appointed guardian who defrauds older clients in *I Care a Lot* and, most recently, the Lucia storyline in season two of *White Lotus*, about a Sicilian sex worker who takes advantage of a tourist's naïveté.

What's interesting is not only how pop culture portrays female con artists but the ways in which gender discrimination shaped their crimes and the story of those crimes. More than tabloid fodder or documentary subjects, their scams are about feminist capitalism, the restrictions placed on female ambition, and how fake-it-until-you-make-it is still largely reserved for the boys. Most of all, they are stories about how we love to see women fail.

To see how gendered grifting can get, let's start with Billy McFarland, a man I like to describe as "if cargo shorts were an actual person." With rapper Ja Rule, McFarland co-founded the infamous Fyre Festival. Scheduled to run over two weekends in April and May 2017, it promised an exclusive concert experience with big-name musical acts like Blink-182 and Major Lazer on the Bahamian island of Great Exuma. Festival marketing included a lavish promotional video that featured famous faces like Bella Hadid and Hailey Baldwin. The video created the illusion that if you attended Fyre, you would be partying on a secluded island with models. As McFarland said in *Fyre: The Greatest Party That Never Happened*, the Netflix doc about the festival, "We're selling a pipe dream to your average loser."

It worked. Organizers sold out the pricey day tickets and festival packages that promised private villas and celebrity chefs. Unfortunately, there wasn't enough planning time and budget to pull off the pipe dream. Fyre lacked room, and toilets, for its 5,000 attendees. There also wasn't enough space for the organizers' egos. "Let's just do it and be legends, man," *The Cut* quoted one Fyre marketer as saying after being presented with a list of challenges the festival faced. When festival goers finally arrived on the island, they found hastily put together FEMA tents left over from Hurricane Matthew in place of luxury villas, a perfect metaphor for the dysfunction, broken promises, and general chaos. If you like mess, this was the music festival for you. There was also no actual music, because most of the acts backed out. Fyre was the number one trending topic on social media for forty-eight hours as attendees tweeted about the fiasco, posting pictures of the festival site, including the now-infamous picture of what unlucky guests were served: processed cheese on sliced bread.

The meme-friendly failure had everything: white millennials with too much money trapped on a secluded island, excessive mocking of Ja Rule, and comparisons to *The Hunger Games*. The jokes may have been funny, but they downplayed the seriousness of the fraud committed by festival organizers, which included stiffing thousands of Bahamian workers out of what they were owed.

Victims don't generally get much sympathy. In January 2019, two documentaries about the festival were released—Netflix's *Fyre: The Greatest Party That Never Happened* and *Fyre Fraud* on Hulu. The documentaries differed in their focus: Netflix explored Fyre's planning, or lack thereof, while Hulu dug into the festival's finances and McFarland's past shady business ventures. (If ever you get confused about the competing films, the Netflix doc was the one where an event planner was persuaded to blow a customs officer to get bottled water released.) The films did, however, have one thing in common: both seemed more interested in bashing the millennials who shelled out money to attend and the influencers who were deceived into promoting the festival. Both groups of people, it's suggested, should have known better. A similar thing happened with Netflix's *The Tinder Swindler* when internet commenters expressed exasperation at the "gullibility" of the women expertly duped by the fake diamond mogul.

The *Fyre Fraud* doc pushed this exculpatory logic to another level. It focused on the societal factors that might have turned McFarland into a con artist: factors which included the way recent entrepreneurial culture has been shaped by the braggadocio, narcissism, and greed of Silicon Valley and Wall Street. But rationalizing McFarland's actions to that extent has the effect of failing to hold him responsible. What it tells us is: McFarland is simply the product of his generation—a generation that, according to *Fyre Fraud*, likes to think big and for which accountability doesn't exist. Don't hate the player, hate the peer group. It's not surprising that this sociological blame game only benefits male fraudsters.

When *Inventing Anna* was released in February 2022, I binged it immediately. The series was entertaining, but its mixture of fact and fiction troubled me. The creative liberties used in telling Delvey's story gave the impression that the details of her life were nothing more than silly putty to be moulded and stretched. Creators might have thought they had agency to do this since Delvey had shaped and bent her own story, but what it meant was that we could never trust the version of events presented on screen.

"This whole story is completely true. Except for all the parts that are totally made up," *Inventing Anna* joked at the start of each of the nine episodes. At first, it was fun to speculate which parts were true and which were fibbed, but it had the effect of turning Delvey into a caricature. "Who the hell is Anna Delvey?" reporter Vivian Kent asked, but we never found out. Delvey was a cartoon party girl in fancy clothes, swishing around New York in her indistinguishable, and much mocked, accent.

Compare this to how documentaries and the press treated McFarland. He was referred to as a "visionary" and a "creative thinker." People talked about how charismatic he was and how he could confidently talk to investors. When Fyre imploded, it was blamed on a lack of capital or a lack of security or poor weather or out-of-control hype but rarely on the sham vision behind it. McFarland and Ja Rule also refused to acknowledge the extent of their damage "We can't dwell on how we fucked up," Ja Rule said in a post-festival team meeting, even going as far as to deflect concerns from employees. "That's not fraud, that's false advertising," he said. Male con artists like WeWork founder Adam Neumann were described in similar ways. These men were not criminals: they were "disruptors." Rather than committing crimes, they were "shaking up the system." Even language is one big con for these men.

Female con artists are rarely afforded such courtesies. Delvey was not a visionary but "a wannabe socialite," or "a fake socialite," or a "dumb socialite." Not surprisingly, she hated these labels. "I was never trying to be a socialite," she told the *New York Post*. "I had dinners, but they were work dinners. I wanted to be taken seriously." Like McFarland, Delvey had a dream. She wanted to build the Anna Delvey Foundation (ADF), a private members' club, featuring an events space, visual arts centre, pop-up shops, restaurant, juice bar, and a bakery. Delvey's vision for ADF started in 2013, when she arrived in New York City posing as the daughter of a diplomat or an oil baron with a massive trust fund she couldn't access because it was housed in international banks.

As it turned out, she was born in Russia and moved to Germany when she was sixteen. She briefly attended a London art school and then interned at a fashion magazine in Paris. Her dramatic reinvention wasn't the act of a vapid party girl but a determined businesswoman— albeit one who stiffed friends for drinks, racked up huge bills at hotels like the Beekman, and tried to settle debts with fake wire transfers.

Female aspirations are constantly belittled, however, and Delvey was no exception. She resented how the district attorney painted her as "a greedy idiot" obsessed with shopping. Coverage of Delvey's wardrobe did little to alter this perception. The *New York Post* breathlessly detailed her fashion choices for her first visit with her parole officer, including mention of an ankle monitor that poked out from designer pants. The *New York Post* also zeroed in on her "heavy eye makeup, high heels, and a black trench coat" and described how she "covered her blow-out with a black head scarf, which was brazenly secured with a broach emblazoned with the initials 'AD.'" For *Glamour*, Delvey was a "fashionable fraudster."

If you ask Delvey, she had no choice. "I have a brand to consider. Also, it's different for women," she said in *Inventing Anna*. Delvey knew that her image was necessary to gain access to business meetings, fancy parties, investors, and exclusive New York society. If ADF was going to be a reality, in other words, she couldn't run around the city in flip flops and hoodies like Facebook's Mark Zuckerberg. "I've been portrayed like I wanted to be famous or I cared about the money and the clothes and whatnot," she told the *Guardian* in 2022. "[I]n fact I was just trying to build a project." Described by *Rolling Stone* as "the chicest woman on trial for grand larceny," Delvey even hired a stylist to assist with her trial looks, and an Instagram account devoted to her courtroom couture currently has 55,800 followers. She knew the publicity the trial would generate and wanted to reflect her brand. In one Instagram post, she referenced what other famous women, from Paris Hilton to Lindsay Lohan, wore in front of a judge. "Going to trial is the new sex tape," she wrote.

Yet one of the interesting points *Inventing Anna* raised was how her look was weaponized against her. Journalists loved to remind us that she was a young woman, implying that she shouldn't be taken seriously. (McFarland was young too, but his age was rarely mentioned, and it's worth noting that he is actually younger than Delvey by almost a year.) "They take one look at my face and my eyes and make assumptions," Delvey said in *Inventing Anna*. In the early years of her scheme, her ex-boyfriend, tech entrepreneur Hunter Lee Soik, helped Delvey gain access to New York's social scene, but she noticed how much easier it was for him to move through the city's elite society and secure support for his own business ventures. Delvey networked, made connections, and promoted her vision for ADF—but she decided against investors. She worried that she would be taken advantage of, that men would cheer her on only to take control of the idea once it launched and was successful. (It's worth taking a moment to say that I do not support or condone the crimes committed by Delvey or any of the con artists mentioned in this piece. Sorry, I should have gotten that out of the way earlier.)

"Through her sheer ingenuity, she created the life that she wanted for herself," Todd Spodek, Delvey's lawyer, said in his opening trial statements. "Anna was not content with being a spectator, but wanted to be a participant. Anna didn't wait for opportunities, Anna created opportunities. Now we can all relate to that. There's a little bit of Anna in all of us." Writing for *Refinery29*, Alice Porter referred to Delvey as belonging to the "antiheros of the girlboss era," citing "their refusal to do the work required to gain the type of success they yearned for." Girlboss, at the time, referred to an ambitious female entrepreneur hustling her way to the top. Delvey might have argued she *was* doing the hard work required. True, much of that girlbossing was criminal. But this was precisely its appeal: she flouted the rules of capitalism.

There was a similar bringing-down-the system take when the movie *Hustlers* was released in 2019. The hit film, which co-starred Jennifer Lopez and Cardi B, was about a group of strippers who steal money from wealthy Wall Street clients. Alex Abad-Santos, in a 2022 *Vox* piece, found similarities with *Inventing Anna* and how the show "operated as a critique against capitalism and the hollowness of the American Dream." All swindler

61

stories illustrate this hollowness, but those involving women—typically more disadvantaged and powerless than men—prove more sharply the differences between the haves and the have-nots.

Jessica Pressler, who wrote the articles that both *Hustlers* and *Inventing Anna* were based on, told *Shondaland* in 2022, "I think that one of the things that's very satisfying about these stories is that when somebody games the system, you see that there *is* a system." Jia Tolentino was more pointed. "Scammers show us the glitzy bullshit intrinsic to stratospheric wealth in America," she wrote in *The New Yorker*. "[T]hey show us that the best way to make money in this country is to treat everyone around you like a mark."

Delvey wasn't the only con lady in my life. There was also Elizabeth Holmes. The media boom her crimes set off included a podcast by ABC News, an HBO documentary, a Hulu series, and a best-seller by the *Wall Street Journal*'s John Carreyrou, whose months-long investigation helped bring down her company.

Holmes founded Theranos in 2003, when she was nineteen. The health-tech company planned to transform diagnostic testing, making it accessible, affordable, and easier by using a finger prick of blood to test for everything from herpes to high cholesterol to cancer. Holmes dropped out of Stanford University, where she was studying chemical engineering, to start Theranos. She was warned by faculty, and others, that her idea wouldn't work and that the technology wasn't possible. That didn't stop her from pursuing investors and partnerships with companies like Walgreens that were planning to launch Theranos's blood-testing technology in their stores. As an attractive, young white woman with confidence and charm, Holmes easily persuaded board members like former US secretary of state Henry Kissinger and investors like Rupert Murdoch that Theranos was successful and that she could be trusted, with little actual data to support her claims. Her messy blonde hair, unblinking blue eyes, unusually (and fake) low voice, and black turtlenecks—the fashion choice of her idol, Steve Jobs—were all part of her con, one she hoped would make Silicon Valley take her seriously.

Holmes's rise was as spectacular as her fall. In 2015, *Forbes* published its inaugural list of the fifty richest self-made women in America. Holmes, the youngest ranked, topped the list. Her blood-testing start-up was valued at $9 billion at the time, and *Forbes* listed her net worth at $4.5 billion. The previous year, she had graced the cover of *Fortune* and was the subject of a lengthy *New Yorker* piece. In 2015, she was one of *Time* magazine's 200 Most Influential People, and that same year, *Glamour* named her Woman of the Year.

One year later, amidst criticisms about Theranos data and technology, and with the company under investigation from various government departments, Holmes's net worth was revised to zero by *Forbes*. In 2018, the US Securities and Exchange Commission charged Holmes with "massive fraud" and bilking investors out of more than $700 million. Her trial ended in early 2022, with the one-time medical entrepreneur sentenced to over eleven years in prison.

One question that kept being raised was whether Holmes believed the Theranos technology would work and was just stalling until it did or whether she knew all along it was snake oil. This fake-it-till-you-make-it ethos is hardly unique to Holmes. It's baked into the very culture of Silicon Valley, where overpromising on a revolutionary idea is often seen as a necessary trick in winning over investors. Start-ups are, in large part, a confidence game, and sometimes the tech being promoted is too good to be true. But sometimes it isn't. And thus a celebrated part of the narrative around Zuckerberg's and Jobs's success—two examples that have given the mantra its power—became suspect the instant Holmes was associated with it. Indeed, one *Washington Post* article, written before the trial, suggested she could be responsible for the downfall of the entire tech world as we know it. "If the court came down hard on her," it read, "it could end the 'fake it till you make it' mantra that seeded so many successful tech firms."

Nothing of the sort is about to happen. The more likely outcome? Women will be punished. Holmes's crimes will reinforce the widely held belief that women can't be trusted and that they're always out to deceive. Silicon Valley CEO Eileen Carey has admitted that she dyes her blonde hair brown in part because she wants to avoid comparisons to Holmes. "It not only can damage her career just individually for herself, but it can actually serve to reconfirm broader cultural beliefs that are out there that women aren't quite the right fit for senior leadership or certain kinds of senior leadership positions," Marianne Cooper, a sociologist at the Clayman Institute for Gender Research at Stanford University, told NPR in a 2016 interview on the chilling effect of Holmes's notoriety on women CEOs. It's always been challenging for women in tech to receive funding. Typically, 2 percent of venture capital goes to women-fronted businesses and start-ups, but post Holmes, the figure is likely to drop. "Holmes was held up as a model for what happens when ambitious businesswomen gain an unprecedented level of investment and trust," Ann Friedman wrote in a 2018 piece on Theranos for *Elle*. "To our great detriment, because of the charges against her, the world may have an answer: They fake it. And now it'll be that much harder for the rest of us to make it."

Of course, one thing that enabled Holmes to get away with her ruse as long as she did was privilege. "Without the armor of their grifts—their thinness, whiteness, and status as blond young women—they would've been immediately labeled con artists," wrote Vanessa Willoughby in a 2019 *Bitch* piece about influencer grifter Caroline Calloway, but the statement could easily apply to Delvey or Holmes. And while their position as white women meant they could keep faking it, they would have been able to keep the game going much longer as a man. McFarland not only faked it until well after Fyre Festival planes had landed on Great Exuma, but he saw the failed 2017 festival as version 1.0 and talked about changes they were going to make for future iterations. "Every day men do far worse things than anything I've allegedly done and what happens to them? Nothing. No consequences. No fallout. And definitely no jail time," said Delvey in *Inventing Anna*. The show featured the character of Alan Reed, inspired by New York real estate lawyer Andrew Lance, who was promoted even though he didn't do due diligence when helping Delvey secure loans to start ADF.

While Holmes's position as a woman in male-dominated Silicon Valley was feted when she was on the rise, it certainly did her no favours when she was caught. We love to see scammers get their comeuppance. But if the runaway sensationalism that drove coverage of Holmes's arrest and trial is any indication, we love it even more when it's a woman.

Delvey seems to be defying the odds, resembling Telfer's Houdini "escaping from one of his famous suspended straitjackets." She was released in February 2021 after serving almost two years in prison. She immediately checked into New York's NoMad hotel and hired a camera crew to follow her around and film her post-prison life. Six weeks after her release, she was taken into custody by Immigration and Customs Enforcement (ICE) for overstaying her visa. After a year in ICE custody, she was supposed to be deported to Germany, but the deportation failed because Delvey refused to get on the plane. A motion to stay her deportation was filed. In October 2022, she was released and remains under house arrest in New York.

Despite being confined to her East Village apartment, Delvey has been busy. There was the "Free Anna Delvey" art show in March 2022. Held at a Manhattan gallery, it included works by artists who were inspired by Delvey's experiences. In May, New York's Public Hotel presented "Allegedly," her first solo show. Since December 2022, she has sold $340,000 worth of art. A dinner party series is in the works, as well as a reality show from Bunim-Murray Productions, the duo behind shows like MTV's *The Real World*. She is also working on a podcast and book, both focused on her life behind bars.

Delvey clearly hopes all of her post-prison activities will allow her to rebrand. "I'd love to be given an opportunity for people not to just dismiss me as a quote-unquote scammer," she told NBC News. I, for one, can't wait for *Re-Inventing Anna*.

Who Deserves Forgiveness?

ON THE MORNING OF November 21, 2022, Chris Brown was trending. He had won an American Music Award (AMA) for Favourite Male R&B Artist the night before. The award capped his record for most nominations in the category, twelve in all. Singer and former Destiny's Child member Kelly Rowland accepted the honour on Brown's behalf but had to tell the crowd to "chill out" after they booed. "I wanted to tell Chris thank you so much for making great R&B music, and I want to tell him thank you for being an incredible performer," Rowland said in her speech. She, too, soon trended on Twitter, with many critical of her support of Brown.

Brown had been slated to perform as part of a fortieth anniversary tribute to Michael Jackson's *Thriller*. The tribute was cancelled at the last minute, and Brown skipped the awards. It was rumoured he couldn't attend because his ex, actress and model Karrueche Tran, would be there, and his presence would violate the five-year restraining order she's had against him. This was the first of two restraining orders she was granted against Brown, who threatened Tran on multiple occasions, punched her in the stomach, and pushed her down a flight of stairs.

Brown has a long history of violent, misogynistic, and homophobic behaviour. The incident he is most known for is his violent attack on singer and then girlfriend Rihanna the night before the 2009 Grammys. The police report and photos from the incident, which left her bruised and bleeding, are both graphic and extremely disturbing. Brown was charged with felony assault and sentenced to five years' probation and 1,400 hours of community service. He was later accused of faking some of his community service and violating his restraining order.

In his 2017 documentary *Welcome to My Life*, Brown discussed the aftermath of the 2009 assault. "I went from being on top of the world, number one songs, being kind of like America's sweetheart, to being public enemy number one," he said in the eighty-minute redemption effort that included performers like Jennifer Lopez, Mary J. Blige, and DJ Khaled.

Brown might have felt like public enemy number one, but his arrests and assault charges hardly dented his career. His label didn't drop him. He's been nominated for more than twenty Grammys, winning one in 2012. He's even had multiple acting stints. As Robyn Autry wrote in a 2021 piece for NBC News, "Some say he's actually benefited from his bad-boy image by branding it as another product for sale."

Brown is not only a best-selling music artist, having sold over 197 million records, but he's also one of the top-grossing Black tour artists of all time. He has the most Billboard 100 entries of any male singer, even surpassing Elvis, and the most top 40 hits of any R&B singer. Brown's collaborations with musicians from Diddy to Justin Bieber to Tory Lanez are proof that plenty of artists are willing to overlook his behaviour. Fellow *Thriller* tribute performer Ciara called Brown "a rare breed of this generation." In October 2022, during a Las Vegas show, Usher brought Brown on stage. "I love you. You a great: You're a legend. We love you and we gon' continue to keep lifting you up," Usher said.

"At this rate," Caroline Sullivan correctly predicted in a 2011 *Guardian* piece on Brown, "there's every likelihood his career will regain its pre-assault momentum, when he was being tipped as the all-singing, all-dancing successor to Usher."

Brown was nineteen when he assaulted Rihanna, and his supporters argue he should be forgiven for something that happened when he was young. "[A] lot of people wouldn't want to see this kid's life messed up over a single stupid mistake. On the most basic level, no man should ever hit a woman, but humans make mistakes," wrote Sullivan. Other defenders argued that Brown was not the type of guy that would punch and kick Rihanna, this despite his long history of violence, while others said she must have provoked him. For a brief period, you could even buy a "Rihanna deserved it" T-shirt on the internet.

But Brown can't seem to help himself. "I think I'm past that in my life," he said of his assault on Rihanna, minutes before a 2011 *Good Morning America* appearance where he trashed his dressing room and broke a window with a chair. He went on to be accused of badly injuring a woman in a San Diego nightclub in 2013 and then was booted from rehab after throwing a rock through the window of his mom's car. His hostility is not limited to women. Also in 2013, Brown used a homophobic slur against singer Frank Ocean while brawling with him.

When *TMZ* caught up with Rowland after the AMAs, she continued to make excuses for Brown. "We all come up short in some sort of way," she said. "And grace is real, and we're all humans. And everybody deserves grace. Period."

When it comes to male celebrities, the media never seems to meet one it couldn't forgive. A few months before the AMAs, the movie *Father Stu* was released. It starred Mark Wahlberg as a boxer turned priest on a journey from self-destruction to redemption. Mel Gibson played his troubled father. Both actors have histories of violent and abusive behaviour. In 1986, Wahlberg was charged with hate crimes after two incidents where he and his friends chased Black children, threw rocks at them, and yelled racial slurs. In 1988, he attacked two Vietnamese-American men, knocked one unconscious, punched the other, and again used racial slurs. He was initially charged with attempted murder, which was reduced to criminal contempt. He was sentenced to two years in prison but served only forty-five days. When Wahlberg's crimes and racism are mentioned, they are usually attributed to his former stage name, Marky Mark. I call this the Eminem clause as it allows you to blame misconduct on an alter ego. Think of it as your own personal Slim Shady. And where do we even start with Gibson? He's been accused of racism, homophobia, antisemitism, and domestic violence. He also seems to have a hard time driving vehicles without being under the influence of alcohol.

Wahlberg and Gibson both got a chance to repair their image. As did Sean Penn and Charlie Sheen. Before he became an ambassador in Haiti, won countless awards, and single-handedly tried to save every Hurricane Katrina survivor, Penn really liked to punch people, mostly photographers, and for years, rumours circulated that he had brutally assaulted his first wife, Madonna. When Penn's bad behaviour is referenced, he's described as "difficult" or a "reformed" bad boy, and the focus is on his film work, not his violent past or—thank god— *Shanghai Surprise.*

Sheen's meltdowns—social media outbursts, drug-fuelled rants—were treated by reporters like a series of hilarious hijinks, while his decades-long history of abuse, harassment, and violence against women was downplayed. Before being fired for his behaviour from the show *Two and a Half Men*, where he basically played a bowling shirt–wearing version of himself, Sheen was television's highest-paid actor, earning a reported $1.8 million per episode.

In 2022, the pop culture moment that topped year-end lists was "the slap." This was when actor Will Smith slapped Oscar host Chris Rock for making a misogynistic joke about Jada Pinkett Smith's shaved head. (She has alopecia, an incurable health condition that causes hair loss.) The slap happened in March, but by the end of the year, Smith was already basking in his redemption: he was all smiles promoting his new film, *Emancipation*.

We never let men suffer for too long before the narrative shifts to how they deserve a second chance. Women are held to a higher standard and punished more harshly. Lindsay Lohan had to wait over a decade for her redemption arc, following a party-girl period in which she crashed her career and reputation. In 2004, Lohan became a household name following the success of *Confessions of a Teenage Drama Queen*, a musical comedy that grossed over $33 million at the box office. That was followed by *Mean Girls*, which earned her rave reviews. That same year came another professional high: Lohan released her debut album, *Speak*, and its first single, the totally fetch "Rumours," reached number one.

Lohan also became a tabloid fixture. A May 2004 cover of *Us Weekly* featured Lohan alongside actresses Hilary Duff and Mischa Barton with the headline "Teens Gone Wild!" It included a story on their "all-night partying" and asked just how out of control young women in Hollywood had become. In the years that followed, Lohan's antics fed the celebrity gossip pipeline. In January 2007, she went to rehab for the first time. Later, she was arrested twice—within a fifty-nine-day period—for driving under the influence, once while in possession of cocaine. Lohan maintained the cocaine found in her pants pocket during the arrest was not hers and that she was wearing someone else's pants (which resulted in "coke pants" entering the pop culture lexicon). By 2010, a *Vanity Fair* piece by Nancy Jo Sales questioned if it was too late for Lohan and whether she would ever recover. "She's Hollywood kryptonite right now," a movie publicist is quoted as saying in the story. "Thanks to her legal troubles (DUIs, mugshots, the works), Lohan's career took a hit. Gone was the teen actress who lit up red carpets for studios like Disney (*The Parent Trap*, *Freaky Friday*) and Paramount (*Mean Girls*), and in her place was a celebrity known more for paparazzi spectacle than acting prowess," wrote Joey Nolfi in *Entertainment Weekly*.

After losing roles because of her reputation, Lohan attempted a return to acting with 2013's *The Canyons*, a microbudget erotic thriller written by Bret Easton Ellis and directed by Paul Schrader, who wrote the screenplays for *Raging Bull* and *Taxi Driver*. Before its release, the *New York Times* reported about the movie's on-set drama, dysfunction, and fights, many of which centred around Lohan. Writer Stephen Rodrick made production sound as painful as going ten rounds in the ring with *Raging*

Bull's Jake LaMotta. Rodrick talked about the concerns Lohan would ruin the film and the careers of everyone involved. "There have been house arrests, car crashes and ingested white powders. His own daughter begs him not to use her. A casting-director friend stops their conversation whenever he mentions her name," it said of Schrader's decision to cast Lohan.

It's worth noting that the *New York Times* piece reminded us of Lohan's past problems without a mention of Schrader's decades-long cocaine addiction that ruined both his career and his first marriage. Ellis, we learned, wasn't keen on casting Lohan because of her baggage, which seemed hypocritical of a man who defended Charlie Sheen. "He's raw now, and lucid and intense and the most fascinating person wandering through the culture," Ellis said of Sheen in a 2011 *Newsweek/Daily Beast* piece. *The Canyons* received negative reviews, but Lohan's role drew praise. In his *New Yorker* review, Richard Brody called her performance "electrifyingly alive," while *Film Comment*'s Kent Jones called her acting "stunning" and "fearless." I was one of the few people who paid to see the movie, and Lohan is definitely the best thing about it. "It's unfortunate, if inevitable, that 'The Canyons' is smothered under the attention that its star, Lindsay Lohan, has been getting for matters other than her acting," wrote Brody.

After *The Canyons*, Lohan tried to get her career and life back on track. It began with the 2014 docuseries *Lohan*, on Oprah Winfrey's OWN Network, which followed Lohan as she attempted to rebuild. Later, there was the 2019 MTV reality show *Lindsay Lohan's Beach Club*, a stint as a judge on season one of the Australian version of *Masked Singer*, and the single "Back to Me," her first new work of music in twelve years. She also moved to Dubai—where paparazzi are illegal—and got married.

In March 2022, Lohan signed a new two-picture deal with Netflix, in which she would both star and executive produce. "The Lindsay Lohanaissance is here!" tweeted *Deadline Hollywood*.

Eight months later, *Falling for Christmas* was released. A movie about a spoiled hotel heiress who gets amnesia after a skiing accident and finds love in a handsome, widowed lodge owner (holiday movies love handsome widowers), it was Lohan's first film in almost a decade. *Rolling Stone* called it a "healthy dollop of Christmas camp" that "marks the first step in the welcome return of Lindsay Lohan." *Variety* praised Lohan's performance and the film, saying its "subversive spirit, female-forward smarts and sweet sentimentality remix the formulaic and festive, making all things merry and bright." A November *BuzzFeed* headline said, "We Really Need To Talk About Lindsay Lohan—Like, She Is A Completely Different Person Than She Was A Few Years Ago."

While I am excited about the Lohanaissance, I also fear her revival has an expiration date not far beyond what's on the carton of milk in my fridge. Women like Lohan are disposable, always one scandal—or so-called scandal—away from being cast out again. Pop culture sets the rules for when women are exiled, when they have appropriately atoned for their sins, and when they are allowed back. Headlines like "Miley is Back!" and "Britney is Back!" herald the *Us Weekly*–sanctioned return of a once-scorned starlet who will now spend the rest of her career on pins and needles, fearful that one small slip will end it all.

There might be no better example of Hollywood's double standard when it comes to forgiveness than Winona Ryder. The actress is best known for her roles in cult classics like *Heathers* and *Beetlejuice* as well as *Mermaids*, *Edward Scissorhands*, and *Girl, Interrupted*. Ryder was nominated for two Oscars, one for *The Age of Innocence*, for which she won a Golden Globe, and the other for her portrayal of Jo March in 1994's *Little Women*. After a series of period pieces, Ryder starred in 1994's Gen X cliché fest *Reality Bites*, which was greenlit only because Ryder was starring.

She became a '90s "it girl," a Gen X icon. Despite her success as an actress, however, Ryder has often been defined by what happened on December 12, 2001, when she was arrested for shoplifting at a Beverly Hills Saks Fifth Avenue store. The items found on Ryder at the time of her arrest totalled $5,500 and included a cashmere Marc Jacobs sweater ($760), Frederic Fekkai hair accessories ($600), and cashmere Donna Karan socks ($80).

While she was detained, police also found various drugs on Ryder, including Demerol, Percocet, and Vicodin. She didn't have a prescription for the drugs, but possession charges were dropped after she provided proof that a doctor had prescribed them. The media speculated Ryder was suffering from a breakdown. She later said she was struggling with depression and was over-prescribed medication that may have clouded her judgment. In November 2002, she was convicted of grand theft and vandalism after a widely publicized trial that focused a lot on what she was wearing. She was sentenced to 480 hours of community service, three years of probation, $3,700 in fines, and $6,355 in retribution to Saks and was ordered to attend psychological and drug counselling.

Over the next few years, Ryder starred in only a handful of roles, which included a guest spot on *Friends*, a cameo in *Zoolander*, and a role in *Mr. Deeds*, which was filmed before her arrest. Rumours circulated that she wasn't working because she was uninsurable. She said she retreated from Hollywood, moved to San Francisco, and focused on other interests. The media didn't like this version of events, which contradicted their fallen/messy-woman narrative, and continued to push the banished-from-movies angle.

"Ryder's meteoric rise to A-List status in her teens and twenties and tabloid-fueled fall shortly thereafter made her a national obsession. But the nearly decade-long hiatus that followed left her tethered to the moment she exited the public eye. America watched her male co-stars—like Ethan Hawke, Christian Slater and Johnny Depp—continue to grow up as they became increasingly bankable movie stars," read a 2016 *Time* piece. It's worth mentioning that two of those three men—Slater and Depp—have had public scandals, including accusations of abuse and harassment of women.

In 2006, Ryder returned to film and starred in *A Scanner Darkly*, *Star Trek*, and *Black Swan* before landing the role of Joyce Byers in Netflix's *Stranger Things*, the supernatural drama. When *Stranger Things* premiered in 2016, the media used the words "comeback," "rebirth," and "resurrection" to constantly remind us of Ryder's downfall. Some headlines also wondered, "What happened to Winona Ryder?" which served as nothing more than an opportunity to revisit all the details of her 2001 shoplifting arrest.

Ryder was unemployable for over a decade for stealing socks, while a man like Brown can beat women and get an American Music Award—an award he is physically unable to accept because of a restraining order.

The most galling example of a celebrity for whom forgiveness was granted at record speed is Shia LaBeouf. In August 2022, *Variety* published a piece on the assault allegations against him. In a 2020 lawsuit, FKA Twigs (real name: Tahliah Debrett Barnett) accused him of sexual battery and physical and verbal abuse. The two dated for close to a year after they met on the sets of the 2019 film *Honey Boy*. "It's a miracle I came out alive," Barnett said in a 2021 *Elle* interview.

LaBeouf denied many of the allegations. "I am not cured of my PTSD and alcoholism. I am committed to doing what I need to do to recover, and I will forever be sorry to the people that I may have harmed along the way," LaBeouf told the *New York Times*. In court documents, Barnett accused LaBeouf of "relentless abuse," which he later referred to as "my failings."

"Over and over again we tell you it is acceptable for men—famous, infamous, or not at all famous—to abuse women," wrote Roxane Gay in 2012. "We look the other way. We make excuses. We reward these men for their bad behavior." LaBeouf has a history of misogyny and violence. Two other women, stylist Karolyn Pho and musician Sia, came forward to support Barnett and talk about the abuse they also suffered at the hands of LaBeouf. In 2015, after an altercation with girlfriend Mia Goth, LaBeouf admitted that if she had not driven away, he would have killed her. In interviews, he claimed he was a changed man after becoming a father and converting to Catholicism. For men like LaBeouf, a sincere, remorseful television interview, a heartfelt *Vanity Fair* cover story, or a trip to rehab is all it takes to rebuild a damaged image.

"We continue to live under the thrall of this idealized standard of perfection for women. Men clearly don't have that," Juliet Williams, a professor of gender studies at the University of California, Los Angeles, said in 2022. No, they clearly don't. As of this writing, LaBeouf has multiple film projects in the works, including one with Francis Ford Coppola.

The Women Who Built Grunge

JENNIFER FINCH IS SMILING, but she's clearly frustrated. "Everywhere I go, everywhere I turn, I see this fucking face," says the bassist for the Los Angeles band L7. "Frankly, I'm sick of it." Finch is holding a copy of the January 1992 issue of *Spin*, which happens to be Nirvana's first national magazine cover; the face in question belongs to her ex-boyfriend, Nirvana drummer Dave Grohl.

The scene appears in the 2016 documentary *L7: Pretend We're Dead*, but the sentiment dates back much farther. When the magazine was published, Finch and her L7 bandmates were in the studio recording their third album, *Bricks Are Heavy*. L7 had formed in 1985, two years before Nirvana was in bloom, and the two bands had toured England together in 1990. Yet, with Nirvana's breakthrough 1991 album, *Nevermind*, Grohl, bassist Krist Novoselic, and lead singer/guitarist Kurt Cobain had seemingly gone from obscurity to ubiquity overnight: *Nevermind* was selling upwards of 300,000 copies a week and was about to knock Michael Jackson's *Dangerous* off the top of the Billboard charts.

Nevermind was not the only seminal grunge album released in 1991. Pearl Jam's *Ten* hit the record store at your local mall in August 1991 and Soundgarden's *Badmotorfinger* in October. By the time L7's *Bricks Are Heavy* was released in April 1992, grunge had exploded: you could buy Soundgarden singer Chris Cornell's look at your local Walmart, rusty cage not included. But as Finch and her bandmates would find, not everyone in the grunge scene was granted the same success; despite glowing reviews, *Bricks Are Heavy* topped out at #160 on the Billboard 200.

From the return of jelly shoes to the pop culture nostalgia of Showtime's *Yellowjackets*, the '90s are back. Chuck Klosterman's latest essay collection, *The Nineties: A Book*, chronicles what the author calls "the last decade with a fully formed and recognizable culture of its own"; *Vice*'s series *The Dark Side of the '90s* revisits the Gulf War, the Viper Room, and the dating history of Counting Crows lead singer Adam Duritz (a Gen X Pete Davidson if ever there was one). And summer 2022 brought thirtieth anniversaries of albums ranging from Sonic Youth's *Dirty* to Screaming Trees' *Sweet Oblivion*—not to mention the *Singles* soundtrack, which packaged the "Seattle sound" for a mainstream audience. Our desire to revisit and re-consume the decade that brought us *Baywatch*, *Beavis and Butt-Head*, and Beanie Babies shows no signs of slowing down.

But not everything is cause for celebration. While the alternative and grunge scene of the early to mid-

'90s celebrated opposition to the mainstream, it was also a very white, very male scene that downplayed the significant contributions of artists who didn't fit that description. Female bands like 7 Year Bitch and Babes in Toyland sold significantly fewer records than their male counterparts, generated fewer bidding wars, and received less press. When not ignored, women were objectified by the media and marginalized by an industry that treated them like a fad, promoting only a handful of female musicians and only for a brief period. As we revisit the decade that gave us grunge, rather than be all apologies, it's the perfect time to re-examine, re-evaluate, and rewrite history—especially for the women who made up the scene.

"If you look at any history of that time, you'd think almost no women were making music," Gretta Harley told *Seattle* magazine in 2013 of Seattle's early grunge music scene. Harley, a punk rock guitarist, had moved to Seattle in 1990 just as grunge was changing the city and putting it on the musical map; she formed the group Maxi Badd (which would become the Danger Gens) with drummer Dave Parnes and bassist Tess. Lotta. But when *Nevermind*'s twentieth anniversary in 2011 prompted a rush of tributes to Nirvana and its influential album, she realized that none of them accurately reflected the Seattle scene—or women's role in it.

That inspired Harley, along with actress and writer Sarah Rudinoff and playwright Elizabeth Kenny, to write the 2013 play *These Streets*. "We started looking at the books that were written by different authors, and the women were absent, almost completely absent," said Harley.

"[W]hen a 250-page history of Seattle's rock heyday … only includes a page and a half on the women of the era—calling it 'The Female Presence'—something feels … wrong," wrote Laura Dannen in a preview of the play for *Seattle Met* magazine. "Like a female guitarist was some kind of elusive Bengal tiger, caught only briefly on tape." *These Streets* explored the experiences of women in grunge in the late '80s and early '90s, drawing on interviews with more than forty women in the scene. From Carrie Akre of Hammerbox and Kim Warnick of The Fastbacks to Lazy Susan's Kim Virant and 7 Year Bitch's Valerie Agnew and Elizabeth Davis-Simpson, *These Streets* shined a light on the contributions that so many histories had ignored.

Even those who managed to break through to wider renown, though, found themselves consistently undervalued. Like Nirvana, L7 had released one of indie label Sub Pop's Singles of the Month, 1990's "Shove/ Packin' a Rod." After its second studio album, 1990's *Smell the Magic*, was also released on Sub Pop, the band signed to Warner Bros. subsidiary Slash Records—for what is described in *Pretend We're Dead* as a "shit deal"— at a time when major labels were scrambling to sign any band with a guitar and proximity to the Space Needle. Even when L7 finally got its own *Spin* cover in 1993, the compliment was backhanded: next to the band's photo was the coverline "More Than Babes in Boyland."

The *Spin* coverline embodied everything L7 was against. It wasn't just sexist; it also manufactured a rivalry between L7 and Babes in Toyland, another female band at the time, flattening both to a girl-group trope. L7 often avoided group interviews and refused to be part of "women in music" special issues because the band felt they deserved their own article and didn't want to be classified by their gender. "When we were naming our band, we did not want a gender-specific name," said singer and guitarist Donita Sparks in a 2012 *Spin* oral history. "I wanted people to listen to our music and go, 'Who the fuck is this?' I didn't really want to be lumped in with anybody. Us being women wasn't a political platform."

The uneven treatment of women in the scene was even more pronounced if you were a woman of colour making music. Tina Bell, a Black woman, formed Seattle band Bam Bam with her husband, guitarist Tommy Martin, in 1983; she was the front woman and principal songwriter. Bam Bam would perform with The Melvins, Soundgarden, and Alice in Chains and were named KCMU/KEXP's "Best NW Band." Its 1984 EP *Villains (Also Wear White)* preceded Green River's album *Come on Down*, often regarded as the first grunge album. Yet, while Bell is often referred to as the "Godmother of Grunge," she's also left out of most histories of the scene.

"This modern genre's sound was, in many ways, molded by a Black woman," wrote Stephanie Siek in a

2021 *Zora* article about Bell's legacy. "The reason she is mostly unknown has everything to do with racism and misogyny. Looking back at the beginnings of grunge, with the preconception that 'everybody involved' was White and/or male, means ignoring the Black woman who was standing at the front of the line."

Bell eventually left the band and quit music; tragically, she died in 2012, shortly before a scheduled reunion of the band. However, when Bam Bam is referenced in accounts of the scene, it is sometimes referred to as a three-piece, removing Bell and her legacy completely. When she does receive a mention, it's often in the context of Kurt Cobain being rumoured to be a fan of Bell and the band. (Cobain had discovered them while he was a roadie for The Melvins.)

Female musicians are often granted legitimacy based on their proximity to more successful male musicians, and Bell is no exception. If you were a woman making music and Cobain name-checked you, you were automatically cool. (Sadly, Courtney Love remains one of the only exceptions to this rule.) "In general, in most histories, women's participation has been disregarded from the get-go or cut from the narrative after-the-fact," wrote Jen B. Larson in a tribute to Bell on the website *Please Kill Me.* "Though women have played key roles in musical innovations over time, we tend to notice them in hindsight, and only if dedicated crate-diggers are meticulous in excavating the past. The motif is especially apparent for Black women."

For a 2016 issue celebrating the twenty-fifth anniversary of grunge, British music magazine *Q* published a special package that included insiders and musicians talking about the scene. Not surprisingly, the piece features no women. Hole's 1994 record *Live Through This* is the only entry from a band featuring women on a list of the twenty-five most influential grunge albums. *Mojo*'s "Early Grunge Classics" and *Revolver*'s "Flyin' the Flannel" both feature no entries by women.

When the media covered women in the grunge and alternative scene, it treated them like a genre unto itself. This genre, though, received almost no in-depth profiles or features. Instead, women were given the listicle treatment: an easy way for an outlet to appear to cover female musicians without the hard work of devoting actual words and thought to them. From "5 Female-Led Bands That Channelled the Fearless Ferocity of Grunge" to "10 Essential Alternative '90s Bands Fronted by Women You Should Know," the facile format signalled that a magazine didn't deem their work or musical contribution worthy of serious consideration.

If music and talent weren't the subject of the listicle, you can probably guess what was: appearance and sex appeal. In 2011, *SF Weekly* somehow managed to use a listicle to objectify women and celebrate male bands at the same time: "As Nirvana's *Nevermind* turns 20 this week, and Pearl Jam celebrates two decades of being a band, we think it's time to look back at the top ten hottest women in grunge," reads the introduction to "The Top 11 Hottest Women in Grunge."

As for the lists themselves, they often highlighted artists who had little in common except their gender. *Diffuser.fm*'s "10 Best Female Rockers of the '90s" includes L7's Donita Sparks, Björk, and Juliana Hatfield—all women, yes, but all women making quite different music. (Garbage and Gwen Stefani on the same list? Why not! They both wrote songs with "Girl" in the title.) Not only do listicles reduce gender to a genre, but they also pit women against each other as they compete for the number one spot—or any spot at all. There are already too many competitive situations for women in music; we didn't need a *Spin* top ten to fuel yet another.

And then there were the "women in music" packages and special issues. These may have devoted more space to the acts in question, but they again flattened these women into a single monolithic group. "The all-women's issue. The women in rock. This ghetto that they put us in. You get the one issue a year. People always compare us to bands with female singers. Not that we don't love those bands, but it seems so narrow-minded to me," said former Sleater-Kinney drummer Janet Weiss in an interview with *Broad City* co-creators Ilana Glazer and Abbi Jacobson.

"Women in music" issues reached their tragic peak in 1997. First came *Spin*'s "The Girl Issue," the cover of which featured Fiona Apple alongside the headline "She's Been a Bad, Bad Girl." Inside, the accompanying profile included this line: "Fiona Apple is a pop star trapped in the body of a pretty teenage girl." (The profile seems

unable to stop reminding readers of Apple's gender, comparing her to other female musicians and repeatedly
talking about her looks and "sexy and girlish" outfits.)
Not to be outdone, *Rolling Stone* published its own "Girl
Issue" later that year, with a cover featuring the random-
seeming combination of Madonna, Courtney Love, and
Tina Turner. Magazines thought they were celebrating
women, without realizing that the very nature of the
celebration accomplished exactly the opposite. Seattle
alt-weekly *The Stranger* punctured the tradition perfectly
with its satirical "men who rock" special issues in 2012
and 2015—complete with sexy-pose photoshoots and
inane interview questions.

When women in the '90s received coverage, interview
questions focused exclusively on the idea that a woman
making music was a novelty. Women were repeatedly
asked to recount tales of the sexism they experienced,
feed into fake feuds with other female musicians, or talk
about their looks, fashion choices, or who they were
dating—all things that would rarely be asked of a man,
except maybe in a parody issue of *The Stranger*. "When
you're a woman working in a man's world, your gender
is acknowledged constantly," wrote Jillian Mapes in a
Flavorwire piece on women rock musicians. "At times
it can feel empowering, this sense of taking up richly
deserved space in a man's world. But at a certain point,
gender-defined underdog status and tokenization grows
old, even if it's positioned as a necessary breath of fresh
air in the press or among fans."

When not objectifying them ("Spanks for the Memory," reads the headline of a 1990 *Melody Maker* piece on Babes in Toyland), coverage focused on female musicians' behaviour over their music. Like L7's Donita Sparks throwing her used tampon into the audience at 1992's Reading Festival after the crowd hurled mud at the band. Or Alanis Morissette talking about going down on a *Full House* cast member in a theatre. Or anything Courtney Love did. ("Love ripped through the grunge scene like a hurricane, marrying its prom king and becoming as notorious for her public antics as for her music," reads the entry for Love on *Diffuser.fm*'s list of the "10 Best Female Rockers of the '90s," which echoed most of the pieces written about her in that decade.)

In the early '90s, grunge was often associated with riot grrrl, the name taken by Olympia, Washington's underground feminist movement. On the surface, the two scenes took a similar form. Both originated in the Pacific Northwest, had their roots in punk, and shared a DIY ethic. Grunge and riot grrrl bands often played shows together, signed to the same record labels, and formed friendships.

But not everyone agreed with the affiliation. "There was a sexist shock-value imagery with grunge," said Allison Wolfe, a member of riot grrrl act Bratmobile, in a 2021 *Guardian* piece on the thirtieth anniversary of the record label Kill Rock Stars. "Especially from Sub Pop bands. It didn't speak to us. I'm not that naked woman on the cover with blood dripping all over me [in Dwarves' 1990 single "Drug Store"]. It was about forging a path to have a voice and knowing even if we didn't have the musical skills that we had something to say that would be more interesting than half the shit these guys are saying."

Female musicians were often labelled by journalists as riot grrrls, regardless of whether they self-identified as such. Not only was it lazy and disrespectful but it also highlighted the limited vocabulary and reference points that existed when talking about women making music. "Riot grrrl" became a catch-all to easily categorize and compartmentalize women.

Meanwhile, riot grrrl bands routinely met with ridicule and dismissal from the media. Rarely, if ever, did journalists or critics engage with the substance of the music. Instead, articles focused on the physical appearances and fashion choices of the girls or wondered whether Chelsea Clinton would become a riot grrrl when she moved to Washington. A *Melody Maker* piece suggested that "the best thing any Riot Grrrl could do is to go away and do some reading and I don't mean a grubby little fanzine," and *Newsweek* called riot grrrl "feminism with a loud happy face dotting the 'i.'"

"I think it was deliberate that we were made to look like we were just ridiculous girls parading around in our underwear," said Corin Tucker, of Sleater-Kinney and Heavens to Betsy, in an interview for *Riot Grrrl Retrospectives*, a 1999 video project by Seattle's Museum of Pop

Culture. "They refused to do serious interviews with us, they misprinted what we had to say; they would take our articles and our fanzines and our essays and take them out of context. We wrote a lot about sexual abuse and sexual assault for teenagers and young women. I think those are really important concepts that the media never addressed." Nowhere was there any mention of the musicians who had influenced riot grrrl acts like Bratmobile and Bikini Kill. It was as though Kim Gordon had never co-founded Sonic Youth, as though The Slits had never existed. Women making music were treated like a novelty—each group of female musicians treated like the first, their history erased and their connection to the future denied. "There were a lot of very important ideas that I think the mainstream media couldn't handle, so it was easier to focus on the fact that these were girls who were wearing barrettes in their hair or writing 'slut' on their stomach," said Sharon Cheslow, who formed Chalk Circle, Washington, DC,'s first all-female punk band in 1981, in another *Riot Grrrl Retrospectives* interview. Riot grrrl eventually declared a media boycott in 1992 over growing concerns that their messages were being misinterpreted, diluted, and trivialized.

And just as with "women in music" special issues, female artists were seen as disposable and automatically compared to each other. "PJ Harvey's record-breaking contributions to indie rock are redoubtable, but rock's one-in one-out policy for women has made her an inescapable comparison for any rock woman standing alone with a six string and toe pressed to a distortion pedal," wrote Charlotte Richardson Andrews in a 2012 *Guardian* piece.

One-in and-one-out also applied to radio airplay and concert bills. If there was already a woman on a festival lineup or in radio rotation in the '90s, there was resistance to adding another. I remember attending Lollapalooza in 1992, disappointed there was only one band featuring women on the bill—British band Lush—especially because the festival prided itself on its diversity. (I also accidentally locked myself in a port-a-potty and missed all of Pearl Jam's performance, which has led to a lifelong fear of both the band and portable toilets, but that's a different piece.)

Lilith Fair launched in 1997 to counter the lack of women on festival lineups and offer support and exposure to female artists—not to mention all the Bioré pore strips audiences wanted. The event grossed $16 million its first year, making it the top-grossing touring festival, but not everyone was happy. "The latest trend in rock and roll: women," announced ABC News's Elizabeth Vargas, opening a segment about Lilith Fair. Sleater-Kinney declined to join Lilith Fair; Garbage's Shirley Manson, among others, criticized it for its lack of diversity. Lilith Fair also helped contribute to the misbelief that music made by women had to be personal, had to be polite, and had to include an acoustic guitar. It also reinforced the idea that women's music is only for women audiences.

Lilith Fair represented a more mainstream, commercial approach to feminism than the political action and activism of the riot grrrls, but both contributed to the idea of the '90s as an encouraging and supportive utopia for female-fronted acts which gave the illusion of gender equality in music. While women musicians achieved undeniable success during the decade, Revolution Girl Style was far from over.

Grunge benefited from its connection to riot grrrl because it made the male-dominated scene seem more feminist, more progressive, and less sexist than it was. When women took Sharpies to their skin, the media dismissed them; when Pearl Jam's Eddie Vedder did it, it somehow became cool and subversive. During a performance of the band's song "Porch" on their 1992 MTV *Unplugged* show, Vedder wrote "PRO-CHOICE!!!" on his arm with a black marker; later that year, he appeared on *Saturday Night Live* wearing a T-shirt with a wire hanger and a pro-choice slogan on it. He also penned a 1992 op-ed on abortion for *Spin*. The mainstream media could handle politics in its music—as long as it was men doing the talking.

Whereas riot grrrl's anger had scared journalists, resulting in misrepresentation and mockery, Vedder was allowed to be angry. "All the Rage," read the cover of *Time*'s 1993 issue about how this new breed of angry male rockers was expressing the "passions and fears of a generation." Both Vedder and Kurt Cobain declined to be interviewed for the story, but Vedder ended up 'on the cover anyway. This trend continued through the '90s: men being lauded for their anger while women like Alanis Morissette were policed for it, accused of manufacturing outrage as a marketing strategy. Female musicians like Morissette had to be just angry enough to sell records, not angry enough to risk offending anyone.

But male grunge bands also promoted a progressive, feminist stance and changed the tone from the machismo and sexism associated with Mötley Crüe and other '80s bands. They helped to bring gender politics to the mainstream and regularly challenged sexism in their song lyrics, interviews, and videos. They championed feminist organizations, causes, and musicians, helping to bring them to a larger, more mainstream audience. I'd grown up watching '80s hair-metal bands on MTV; male musicians promoting the idea that women were something other than bangable flesh trophies blew me away more than a Ratt video's pyrotechnics ever could.

In interviews, Cobain regularly supported and name-checked female musicians, from Shonen Knife to The Breeders, expanding the audience for these artists. In some cases, as with L7, these bands had been making music for longer than Nirvana, but unfortunately, it took a man championing them to bring the girls to the (fore)front. Cobain and Vedder also supported female musicians by bringing them on tour or joining them on the bill for benefits in support of a variety of causes, including Rock for Choice and Rock Against Rape. I remember a male friend praising Vedder for organizing Rock for Choice.

95

He assumed the singer was responsible for it after he saw a picture in a music magazine of Vedder sporting a shirt for the benefit concerts. (He didn't; that was L7 and Sue Cummings, a senior editor for *LA Weekly*.) Bands ranging from Rage Against the Machine to Mudhoney played Rock for Choice concerts during the '90s, and while Vedder wearing the shirt helped to raise the cause's profile, it also overshadowed the important work L7 and other female musicians did.

What's often overlooked, and important to remember, is that female musicians influenced Cobain's feminist message—notably, Bikini Kill's Kathleen Hanna and Tobi Vail—as did the formative time Nirvana spent in Olympia. Cobain's activism didn't come from nowhere; it came from his proximity to, and association, with riot grrrl. "From the very beginning, he was aware of the gender issue," said NPR music critic Ann Powers in a *Daily Beast* story about Nirvana's legacy. Cobain may have promoted Bikini Kill and riot grrrl in interviews, but he wouldn't have had his feminism without them.

This year marks the twenty-ninth anniversary of Cobain's death. Each year, the music media commemorates the occasion with tribute articles, think pieces, and reminders of all the conspiracy theories that still surround Cobain's death. "10 Years After His Tragic Death: Why The Man And His Music Still Matter" reads the cover of an April 2004 issue of *Spin*. The "special collector's issue" includes a history of grunge, a list of thirty essential Nirvana recordings and other media, and musicians ranging from The Strokes to Soundgarden sharing their memories of Cobain. Similar tributes mark the anniversary of the deaths of Soundgarden front man Chris Cornell, who died by suicide in May 2017, and Alice in Chains singer Layne Staley, who died of a drug overdose in April 2002.

Sadly, the deaths of female musicians don't receive nearly the same level of media attention. The death anniversary of Mia Zapata, lead singer of The Gits, who was murdered and brutally raped in July 1993, deserves more tributes. The deaths of Hole bassist Kristen Pfaff, who died two months after Cobain, or 7 Year Bitch lead guitarist Stefanie Sargent, who died in 1992, should also not be overshadowed by the deaths of male musicians.

Deaths are not the only occasions that are marked. When *Nevermind* turned thirty in 2021, the anniversary was marked by special commemorative issues of *Uncut* and *Mojo*. There was a thirtieth anniversary reissue box set, online tributes, social media shoutouts, and an endless-seeming parade of dudes telling you where they were the first time they heard "Smells Like Teen Spirit." Similar tributes happened with the album's 10- and 20-year anniversaries. When we think about nostalgia, it's important to notice whose legacy is remembered, who gets the anniversary covers, whose cultural significance is celebrated—and whose isn't.

Grunge is far from the only musical scene to marginalize women's contributions. In a 2014 *Guardian* article about the punk scene's misogyny, writer Charlotte Richardson Andrews argued that women had to fight for visibility in a scene where men held all the power. Women were too often excluded from an industry that only promoted "the lucky few to whom industry gatekeepers deign to give a platform." The piece could just have easily been describing grunge.

Or hip-hop, for that matter. Starting in the late '80s, female hip-hop artists like Queen Latifah and MC Lyte achieved undeniable success. In 1988, Salt-N-Pepa's "Push It" was one of the first hip-hop singles to be nominated for a Grammy. Latifah's most successful album, 1993's *Black Reign*, was certified gold, and its Grammy-winning single "U.N.I.T.Y." explicitly celebrated women's rights. Their music defined the genre as they spoke out against assault, discrimination, and misogyny. But like women in grunge, this perspective didn't receive as much attention as it should have: songs like "Ladies First" existed within a male-dominated genre and culture where, as Jeff Chang wrote in *Can't Stop Won't Stop: A History of the Hip-Hop Generation*, "scantily-clad dancers seemed in endless supply, while women rappers were scarce." At least in grunge, Eddie Vedder wasn't pulling a 2 Live Crew and singing about someone blowing him, as much as he may have wanted Ticketmaster to.

In 1999, *Billboard* named pop singer Mariah Carey the artist of the decade. For those who had grown up with grunge, it seemed a fate worse than whatever Y2K had planned. By then, grunge bands were long gone, replaced by mass-produced boy bands and pop princesses as well as the burning (literally) mess that was Woodstock '99. Riot grrrl's girl-power message had been co-opted and commercialized to sell pencil cases and baby tees. Smelling like teen spirit had been replaced by actual teen spirit as preteen girls flocked to the Backstreet Boys, NSYNC, and the Spice Girls.

But, thankfully, yesterday's pioneers refuse to stay in the background. After six studio albums, L7 went on an indefinite hiatus in 2001—only to reform in 2014 and tour with its original lineup for the first time in twenty years. In 2022, they toured again to celebrate the thirtieth anniversary of *Bricks Are Heavy.* Sleater-Kinney, who released their tenth studio album, *Path of Wellness*, in 2021, also returned to the stage. Sonic Youth's Kim Gordon is back with *This Woman's Work: Essays on Music*, an anthology she edited with music journalist Sinéad Gleeson. "'What's it like to be a girl in a band?' The often-repeated question throughout my career as a musician made me feel disrupted, a freak or that we are all the same," wrote Gordon in an Instagram post promoting the book. "I once asked my boyfriend what it was like to have a penis? To me they are sort of equivalent questions. Hopefully, this book begins an unravelling of this myth that if you're a female musician you are ready-made, easily digestible."

It's long overdue.

OCD is Not a Joke

WITH MY BRACES AND SUN In bleached bangs, I may have looked like every other teenager at my 1980s suburban junior high, but I knew something about me was different. I was thirteen when I first noticed myself acting in ways that resembled obsessive-compulsive disorder (OCD), though I wouldn't have known to call it that at the time. It was the summer before ninth grade, the era of coming-of-age movies like *St. Elmo's Fire* and *The Breakfast Club*. My girlfriends and I were obsessed with Brat Pack actors like Emilio Estevez, Judd Nelson, and Rob Lowe. We spent our babysitting money and allowances at the local Red Rooster, buying slushies (half Coke, half cream soda) and magazines. At sleepovers, we pored over *Teen Beat* and *Bop*, spending hours discussing what *The Outsiders* star Matt Dillon was looking for in a girl or deciding which actor's shirtless centrefold we would hang in our locker once school started.

We rode our ten-speeds around our suburban Edmonton neighbourhood well past curfew, quizzing one another on the actors' heights and favourite books.

I could never remember my locker combination, but I knew, down to the inch, how tall Rob Lowe was. We took the number 33 bus to and from West Edmonton Mall to see *St. Elmo's Fire* so many times we could essentially recite the whole movie. I imagine the bus driver was relieved when *Weird Science* came out later that summer: it gave us some new material to act out on the ride home.

I wouldn't say loving John Hughes characters was obsessive behaviour, exactly—or at least no more obsessive than that of any other teen girl I knew. But I would bet a Judd Nelson glossy eight-by-ten that I was the only girl in my friend group who was both confused and troubled by the need to wake up several times a night to check on the pile of *Teen Beats* on her bedside table. My nighttime ritual consisted of making sure none of the magazines' pages had accidentally folded over or been damaged during my pre-bedtime reading and stacking. I would lift each magazine up, inspect it to make sure it was in perfect shape, and replace it on the pile—which had to be in a certain corner of my nightstand, right between my Cabbage Patch Kids doll and Dr Pepper Lip Smacker.

Thirty-nine years later, my checking behaviour continues—only it's no longer Brat Pack centrefolds that consume me. Checking is a common OCD ritual, right up there with counting, tapping, cleaning, and hand-washing. It's also what people often, mistakenly, think all forms of OCD look like. In the US, nearly one in 100 people suffer from OCD, with about half of those cases being severe. In Canada, 1 percent of the population will experience an episode. I am one of these Canadians. I lose hours of every day to various checking rituals—making sure my bathtub tap isn't dripping, or my hair straightener is off, or my apartment door is locked.

Most people with clinical OCD have both obsessions and compulsions, but the compulsions—the counting, the checking, and so on—are typically the focus when the condition appears in entertainment or popular media. Compulsions on screen are often played for laughs, like *Parks and Recreation*'s Leslie Knope's fondness for three-ring binders and colour coding or Bill Murray's baby step–obsessed character in the 1991 film *What About Bob?* A friend recently sent me a list of celebrities who have OCD, or what journalists think OCD looks like—it included the fact that Cameron Diaz opens doors with her elbows. The *Wall Street Journal* recently used the headline "We All Need OCD Now" for an article on COVID-19 and the importance of frequent handwashing. Finally, my debilitating mental illness has a timely hook!

The obsessions—the unbidden thoughts driving the compulsions—are comparatively less discussed. When I try to explain my OCD to people, they don't understand the fears and anxieties that drive these compulsions or what the repeated actions are meant to accomplish. I don't check taps because I am really into ornate faucet design. I do it because it is the only way to quiet my brain.

I once heard OCD described, very accurately, as a record skipping in your head. The checking routine I have before I leave my apartment can take anywhere from thirty minutes, on a very good day, to two hours, on a very bad one. There is a voice in my head that won't go away, repeating: "You must check the fridge door to make sure it is closed, or the fridge will defrost. All your food will go bad and your kitchen will flood. It will destroy your apartment and the one below it." I pray that my foot won't hit the overflowing recycling bag in my kitchen that sits directly across from the fridge. If my foot hits it, it disrupts my very specific, everything-in-its-place checking routine, and I have to start all over again. Repeatedly checking the door helps to calm all the fears I have about what disasters could happen if the door were left open. These fears may seem irrational, even ridiculous, to others, but they are very real to me.

My OCD makes me feel like a bad friend, a bad co-worker, and a bad daughter. I can't show up places on time and I feel like I am always apologizing for being late. I can't travel easily and I avoid doing so whenever I can. If I do have to travel, I start dreading it months in advance. My pre-leaving-my-apartment routine is nothing compared to my routine for leaving my apartment for a vacation. I often cancel plans so I can avoid having to leave my house at all—the thought of going through my checking is too exhausting to contemplate.

As a result, I isolate myself. I live in fear of people laughing at me, which they have done. I avoid relationships because I can't imagine someone staying at my house for a night. "Just go to bed. I'll be there in a couple of hours, after I check the windows repeatedly to make sure they are closed because I am worried that, if they aren't, someone will somehow scale the side of my building, climb three floors, cut the window screen, and enter the bedroom to kill us."

Who's in the mood for romance now?

Media and pop culture portrayals of OCD don't help with the misconceptions about it. People with OCD are typically portrayed as type A clean freaks, Sheldon Cooper–like nerds, productivity machines, or eccentric weirdos. In case you're wondering: no, I don't wear tissue boxes on my feet like Howard Hughes. No, I don't have an elaborate floor-cleaning process like Faye Dunaway in *Mommie Dearest*. No, I don't spend all day avoiding cracks in the sidewalk like Jack Nicholson in *As Good as It Gets*.

Stereotypical portrayals too often focus on the rituals and portray none of the nuanced, often agonized thinking behind them. Consequently, it's become common—and even acceptable—for anyone who likes things in order or who keeps a clean house to use the OCD label to describe themselves.

"I'm so OCD" has become a joke, a shorthand for being clean or organized. The first time I noticed this, I was sitting in a work meeting watching the woman across from me remove pencils from a case and arrange them neatly in a row in front of her. "I'm so OCD," she joked when she caught me watching her. No one else seemed to notice what she was doing. I asked her if she had OCD; she confessed she didn't. She told me she just liked her pencils in colour-coded order. I blame shows like *Friends* for making her think it's okay to treat OCD like a quirk—like being Monica Geller–level organized is the same as having a debilitating illness.

The actual suffering of those with OCD has been replaced by puns and punchlines. There are "Obsessive Crossfit Disorder" shirts—if only my suffering was healthy and came with increased stamina. Retail giant Target even had an "Obsessive Christmas Disorder" sweater, for which it was later criticized. (If Christmas isn't your thing, I also recently discovered "Obsessive Cookie Disorder" versions.) There is also something called "Obsessive Castle Disorder," which is used to describe fans of the Nathan Fillion crime drama *Castle* and, sadly, not people who enjoy actual castles.

It seems like marketing departments can't get enough of my mental illness. My inbox often fills with listicles and quizzes like "33 Meticulous Cleaning Tricks for the OCD Person Inside You" and "5 Types of OCD Friends You Know and Love." I have had people joke that I should bring my OCD over to their place so I can clean their home, as if my mental illness were a bottle of Javex. On the television drama *Monk*, detective Adrian Monk uses his OCD to help solve crimes, and Khloé Kardashian recently talked about how her OCD, which she's never confirmed a diagnosis of, helps her to create perfectly stacked rows of Oreos and closets with clothing organized according to colour and type. She refers to it as her "KHLO-C-D" and has turned it into a money-making venture, with sponsored posts on her Instagram feed that show her surrounded by bedazzled bottles of Febreze. She would be the perfect contestant on *Obsessive Compulsive Cleaners*, a UK reality show that has shown people diagnosed with OCD team up to clean dirty homes. Pop culture portrayals like this make OCD look like a blessing, not a curse.

I have many criticisms of the HBO show *Girls*, from its lack of diversity to pretty much the entire character of Marnie, but Hannah Horvath's OCD in season two was the closest thing I've seen to a realistic onscreen depiction. Show creator Lena Dunham has talked openly about her own OCD and anxiety, on which Hannah's experiences are based, and her desire to end the stigma around it. Mercifully, Dunham didn't make OCD Hannah's defining personality trait—a relief for people like me who are sick of portrayals that do just that. (As we all know, it's being a total narcissist, not having OCD, that is Hannah's defining trait.)

In the show's second season, we see Hannah take eight potato chips out of a bag and line them up neatly in a row on her kitchen table. She scoops them up and shoves them in her mouth, chewing them eight times before swallowing. More things are done in eights: she blinks eight times and opens and closes her front door eight times before entering her apartment. She repeats "You are fine and good" eight times to herself in front of the hotel mirror. When the counting takes over, she is unable to do much else apart from giving herself a bad haircut and eating a tub of Cool Whip. The stress of a looming deadline and a recent breakup only makes it worse.

Hannah eventually visits a therapist and describes the exhausting nature of her rituals: how they keep her up until the wee hours and how they make her feel like a zombie in the morning. When I first saw this episode, I felt like she was describing my situation. I was so relieved to finally recognize myself in an OCD portrayal that I burst into tears and sat on my couch sobbing until well after the episode had ended. I had a similar reaction to HBO's *Euphoria*, which also offers an accurate and honest portrait of living with OCD.

It isn't just the lack of positive pop culture portrayals of OCD that makes me feel bad. I recently watched an old episode of *Sex and the City* where Carrie Bradshaw is getting ready to leave on a trip. She finishes her cigarette, gently stubs it out in an ashtray, grabs her luggage, and leaves her apartment. I don't know what happened next because I was unable to focus on the rest of the episode. I kept thinking: "Is that cigarette properly out? There is no way that gentle stub could have extinguished it. She didn't even really check it. What if her apartment burns down?" I wondered if she would worry about it later. Would she be unable to properly focus on her

conversation with Samantha about big dick energy—
this was pre–Pete Davidson—or Mr. Big?

If that had been me, I would have had to flush the
cigarette butt, rinse the ashtray numerous times, and
leave it filled with water in the sink. After those steps, I
would have taken numerous pictures of the ashtray with
my cellphone in case I was worried later about whether
my cigarette was, in fact, out. My OCD was ruining *Sex
and the City* for me—something I thought only the
Aidan storyline was capable of.

I recently realized that I went three months without
using my stove, reasoning that, if I never turned it on,
then I didn't have to worry about checking it. If food
needed to be heated, I microwaved it or used boiling
water from a kettle, or else I didn't eat it at all. That lasted
until I began to think about checking the microwave
and kettle, at which point I switched to sandwiches and
cereal. My OCD has cost me so many moments and
opportunities.

I dread my morning checking routine so much
that I stay in bed well past my alarm, thinking of all
the rituals that must be done. I lie in bed for as long as
I can, staring at my bedroom ceiling, listening to my
upstairs neighbour race around in the morning. I live
in an old building, where every floorboard creaks and
every footstep echoes. I can tell my neighbour's morning
routine takes her under an hour, and I envy her for it.
But I'm also resentful, and not just because she appears

to love wearing clogs. I so badly want to be someone who can run out the door in the morning, someone who grabs their keys and just goes.

Before the pandemic, when I still worked in an office, I avoided early morning work meetings because I couldn't even imagine what time I would have to wake up to make it somewhere for 9 a.m. Instead, I'd have a list of excuses ready, from the specific "dentist" to the vague "prior meeting," but rarely were any of them true. I am very blessed to have incredibly understanding co-workers and a job, as the publisher of a small progressive magazine, that did not require me to be at my desk from nine to five.

But, as blessed as I am, I still wanted to make morning meetings, and I constantly felt like a failure when I couldn't. I wanted to be one of those people who stops at the café by their office every morning to have granola and fruit and to read the paper before their workday begins. I long to be one of those writers who works for two hours in the morning before stepping foot in the shower. But I cannot. For starters, I would have to turn on my laptop— and that would require adding its status to the already too long list of things I have to check.

By the time I'd get on the subway for my commute to work, I would already be exhausted. I'd wait in my apartment, sweating in my coat as I looked out my peephole and listened until I heard my neighbours exit the hall. I didn't want anyone to see me standing in front of my apartment door, checking and rechecking the lock, pushing on the door, putting my purse and tote bag down on the floor so I can push with both hands. I dreaded someone seeing me get halfway down the hallway only to turn around to check it all over again.

When my OCD is at its worst, I think of all the things I do in a day as just noise and static sandwiched between checks—no matter how important or fulfilling they might be at other times. Back in the office, which had a whole different checklist than my apartment, I'd often work late, well past the hour when I should have stopped, just to avoid starting the routine at the end of the day.

When the voice in my head is not telling me that I must check the stove repeatedly to make sure it's shut off or my apartment will catch fire, the voice tells me I am imperfect—I am a failure because I cannot silence it. So I push myself to work harder, to do better, and to achieve more. I am so disappointed in myself that I channel that frustration into a near impossible level of perfectionism. Stress only makes it worse. When there are things I can't control, I focus on my compulsions— which sometimes feel like the one thing I can control.

One thing I know I can't control are the long, daunting wait lists to get mental health treatment. I have been on many lists for more years than Khloé Kardashian has been arranging Oreos. Once a person does access help and support, it can be prohibitively expensive to maintain it. I did save a lot of money eating sandwiches and cereal for months, but even that wasn't enough to afford help. A typical therapy session in Toronto, where

I live, can cost up to $175 an hour. Online resources can help only so much. And it can be difficult to navigate and maintain a potential support network of friends and family. While I try to be open about my OCD, I have shared in the past only to be told that I should "get over it" or "just stop," as if it were that easy. I also had a friend who used to regularly give me CDs by artists with OCD, like Fiona Apple and Joey Ramone. I assume this was meant to be a form of help, but I had no idea what I was supposed to do with these. A musical interlude?

Long wait lists for help need to end, but so do unrealistic pop culture portrayals. Accurate representations—ones that include both the obsessions and the compulsions—increase our understanding of the condition and, in turn, make people like me feel more comfortable talking about it without worrying about being mocked or reduced to a stereotype.

Jennifer Aniston Gives
Birth to Teenager!

SIXTEEN. THAT'S THE NUMBER of years tabloid magazines spent declaring Jennifer Aniston pregnant. Rumours started gestating when the actress was still married to Brad Pitt, five years before their divorce in 2005, but really ramped up post Pitt. Aniston was "pregnant and alone," "pregnant with twins," "pregnant with John Mayer's baby"—your body is not a wonderland when that happens—and a "pregnant bride." She's been pregnant in every possible situation, except the one where she is actually with child.

In June 2016, *In Touch* published a cover story declaring "Jen's finally pregnant," complete with photos of Aniston and husband Justin Theroux on their Bahamas babymoon. (Please make this word go away forever, I beg of you.) In what felt like a 100-page article, the tabloid discussed possible baby names, nursery plans, and what she is eating now. She has a special salad! It has feta!

The photos that accompanied the piece painfully dissected Aniston's body, with arrows pointing to her baby bump and illustrating how her body is getting "fuller." In case the close-ups of her midsection weren't enough to convince readers, *In Touch* pointed out a picture of Theroux paddling a floating thingy around some water. The magazine emphasized that Jen was not paddling, because everyone knows pregnant women don't paddle. The photos also looked more like she had maybe just skipped the special salad that day and had a burrito instead. Burrito or baby bump? You decide! (I will always side with team burrito.)

Aniston didn't seem to enjoy the cover story, or the last sixteen years of them, and soon after penned an essay for *Huffington Post* confirming she was not pregnant and calling out tabloids for using "celebrity 'news' to perpetuate this dehumanizing view of females, focused solely on one's physical appearance." She went on to criticize the magazines for defining "a woman's value based on her marital and maternal status" and for perpetuating "this notion that women are somehow incomplete, unsuccessful, or unhappy if they're not married with children."

Responses to Aniston's piece ranged from "How brave!" and "You go, girl!" to criticism that she has no right to rail against the magazines when she is part of the ridiculous Hollywood machine that promotes unrealistic and unattainable standards of beauty. Online commenters called her a hypocrite for shaming tabloids for focusing on her looks when she makes millions endorsing beauty products. Aniston, at the time, shilled for Aveeno and smartwater, both of which seem harmless enough. Or wait—maybe you're right, dear anonymous internet commenter: an insistence on moisturizing or staying hydrated totally gives me a right to her uterus.

Keeping it classy, others commented on her appearance. It's helpful to respond to an essay about body shaming by pointing out that someone looks like Jay Leno with a potato stuck in the middle of their face. Thanks "feminist" website. Women's magazines applauded Aniston for her stand but then seemed to cling desperately to the part of the piece where Aniston admits, "Yes, I may become a mother someday."

Others used the essay as an opportunity to talk about Aniston's acting skills. I am not a huge fan of *Friends*, but that's not the point. I may not be hanging out at Central Perk, but I (and many other non-celebrity women) can relate to feeling interrogated about not reproducing. Aniston is over forty, which makes the media even more uncomfortable with her decision to not embrace motherhood. I am three years younger than Aniston and have, unfortunately, run into this all the time. At a recent work meeting, a woman I had just met asked if I had children. When I responded that I had no desire to, she looked at me like I had just asked the group to blue-sky a large pile of human feces I had left in the middle of the boardroom table. (She also took the last muffin, so she's basically a monster all around.)

The tabloids have focused so much on Aniston's stomach over the years I feel like I could now confidently pick it out of a police lineup. George Clooney married and had children late in life, according to celeb gossip standards, but I have never seen a paparazzi close-up of the Ocean's Eleven in Clooney's pants with the headline "Full of baby batter or just awkward-fitting Dockers?" Also, Clooney's decision to marry later in life made him a desirable "bachelor" and "hard to lock down," while Aniston's made her a sad, lonely woman who was going to die alone surrounded by cats and/or burritos.

When Aniston wasn't on twenty-four-hour bump watch, she was busy feuding with Angelina Jolie. A 2016 cover story declared the two had an "Explosive Showdown." Apparently, Pitt sent Aniston an email offering condolences on the recent death of her mother, and all hell broke loose. (Did she die watching Pitt and Jolie's movie *By the Sea*, because that thing sounds so awful it's basically like the videotape in *The Ring*?) Sadly, this cover story is not new. Rachel Green and Mrs. Smith had been going at it—and not in the way the majority of people would like them to—since 2005. When these ladies started feuding, George W. Bush was still president of the US and Facebook was barely a year old. Let that sink in for a moment.

From celebrity boob blunders to celebrities without makeup to who wore it best, the tabloids are constantly scrutinizing, analyzing, and pitting women against each other. In 2016, *Star* featured a report on Hollywood's best and worst moms, complete with scores for each. Jolie gets an A+, which is amazing since, according to the tabloids, she spends all her time engulfed in a seemingly never-ending episode of *Cheaters*. Courtney Love gets an F. As a defender of Love, even I'll admit she probably won't win any PTA awards, but I'd like to point out that in *Kurt Cobain: Montage of Heck*, she is the only parent of Frances Bean not shown nodding off on heroin while holding her and is also the only parent—spoiler alert—still standing at the end of the film.

The tabloids have yet to release, and probably never will, their rankings of Hollywood dads. They rarely discuss this. They used to talk about how Tom Cruise doesn't see his daughter Suri, but that's because he is a weird Scientologist, not because he is a man. There is no celebrity boner blunder coverage and rarely do men make the worst bodies' issue, which is the tabloids' answer to the swimsuit issue. Mickey Rourke occasionally washes up on the beach, but that's about it.

When tabloids mention dads at all, it's usually to praise them for simple things like just being in the same room as their offspring. Even Charlie Sheen's parenting skills have been applauded. A story about him mentioned his great relationship with his kids, despite what must be the scores of child psychologists circling them like vultures, visions of billable hours dancing in their heads.

But trashy tabloids aren't the only ones at fault. *Vanity Fair*, in 2016, came under criticism for an August cover story on actress Margot Robbie. Writer Rich

Cohen basically spends the piece nursing a journalistic hard-on for Robbie, and the result is a sexist, offensive piece, sparking writer Roxane Gay to tweet: "Every issue of *Vanity Fair* this month comes with a thin sheen of Rich Cohen's semen holding the pages of Margot Robbie's profile together."

The classic defence is that editors are just giving readers what they want. According to an *Adweek* report, what readers want is Aniston. Her July 2015 *Life & Style* "It's Official! Jen is…Finally Married!" (phew!) cover was the magazine's best-selling issue of the year and sold more than 260,000 copies. Her post-Pitt 2005 *Vanity Fair* cover remains one of the magazine's top five covers of all time. Speculation about Aniston's womb is newsstand gold.

And gold it has stayed.

Tabloid coverage of Jennifer Aniston and her uterus has intensified in the intervening years. In 2022, she was in the news again and, not surprising, it had to do with kids, or her lack of. For decades, tabloids have portrayed Aniston as a sad, single childless lady who sits alone in her Hollywood mansion working on her Jolie burn book.

A March 2022 *Us Weekly* cover asked, "What's Wrong With Jen" and mentioned her being "trapped & alone in a '$50 million prison'" and "her personal crisis over plans for a baby." In November, *Us Weekly*'s cover promoted "Jen's Untold Story" and talked about her up-coming memoir that would reveal "her REAL feelings about her exes." A few weeks earlier, headlines had her romancing her *Morning Show* co-star Jon Hamm, who sources said she had a crush on for years. Get those Skip the Dishes coupons, Jen! Also, remember that summer the internet was obsessed with his junk and nicknamed it "Hammaconda"?

Post Pitt, Aniston dated a series of high-profile men, from singer John Mayer to actor Vince Vaughn, and the tabloids were there for every *Vanity Fair* Oscar Party photo op and poolside make-out session. After she wrote that 2016 *Huffington Post* editorial, she divorced her second husband, Theroux, starred in *The Morning Show*, her first television role since *Friends*, and won a Screen Actors Guild Award, in addition to receiving Emmy and Golden Globe nominations, launching haircare line LolaVie, starring in movies, and crashing Instagram when she joined the platform and posted a *Friends* reunion photo.

In December 2022, she appeared on the cover of fashion and beauty magazine *Allure*'s final issue, and motherhood came up in the interview, but this time she controlled the narrative, and when the issue was published, things got weird (weirder than her starring in *Leprechaun*). The cover featured Aniston in a Chanel micro bikini top (apparently called a "nipplekini"), accompanied by the line "I don't have anything to hide at this point."

She talked about her struggles to conceive over the years. "It was a challenging road for me, the baby-making road," she said. "All the years and years and years of speculation… It was really hard. I was going through IVF, drinking Chinese teas, you name it. I was throwing everything at it. I would've given anything if someone had said to me. 'Freeze your eggs. Do yourself a favor.' You just don't think it. So here I am today. The ship has sailed." It was something Aniston had never talked about, but many women could likely relate.

Aniston also discussed the decades-long narrative that she was selfish, that she didn't want children because she was too focused on her career, and that her husband left her because she prioritized making movies over making babies. So, of course, the internet read the *Allure* story and responded with kindness and sensitivity. Kidding! The coverage was only slightly less offensive than *Friends* co-star Matthew Perry wishing Keanu Reeves dead in his 2022 memoir. Aniston was finally opening up about something the media had speculated about for years, but they didn't want to discuss it on her terms, because it didn't fit the narrative of Jen as sad, single, and lonely. She had made peace with herself, but no one wanted that. Instead, they preferred the version of events they had constructed for her.

Coverage mentioned the IVF story but quickly moved on to Aniston's looks and age. "In the accompanying images," wrote *Slate*, "Aniston bared *a lot* of what women's magazines would call her bod: boobs beneath a pair of round pastie-like coverings by Chanel, a backside in low-rise pants and a Gucci G-string, the side of her thigh in a dress that she pulled down with her thumbs." This bod, *Slate* was quick to remind readers, belonged to a woman over fifty. *Slate* was not alone in referencing Aniston's age. *Gawker* shamed Aniston for showing most of her boobs on the cover. The image, they wrote, "makes her look like she's wearing a Julia Fox costume but forgot to do the eye makeup." They didn't stop there. "The whole photoshoot is a bizarre exercise in seemingly trying to convince us that Jennifer Aniston, famously beautiful woman, is still hot." Piers Morgan also entered the chat and tweeted a picture of the cover and called it tacky. Coming from the man who once edited the British tabloid the *Daily Mirror* and competed on *The Apprentice*, that call is coming from inside the house, Piers.

Critics of the *Allure* cover talked about the obvious photoshopping and how dangerous that can be to a woman's self-esteem, especially for younger women. Yes, photoshopping is harmful, but criticizing the beauty industrial complex and then, a few sentences later, mocking Aniston for showing her body (some social media commentators called the cover "soft porn") and criticizing her fashion choices is hardly good allyship. And when critics weren't scandalized about the photoshopping, they were obsessed about whether Aniston had plastic surgery. This is a very common fixation when women in Hollywood over the age of thirty appear on a magazine cover—or simply decide to leave their house and interact with the outside world. Did she? Didn't she? The relentless debate about Aniston's alleged facelift was exhausting to follow, and each piece treated her like some smartwater-swilling Benjamin Button tricking time with technology.

Look: Aniston is extremely wealthy and has access to the best personal trainers, personal chefs, photographers, and plastic surgeons. Hers is definitely a beauty that is unattainable to the average person. This is important to remember, but should it be the focus of *every* piece about her? Also, please stop talking about how brave it is when an older woman dares to grace the cover of a fashion magazine in something other than a *Golden Girls*–style caftan.

There was another female celebrity over the age of fifty who graced a magazine cover in December 2022. When *Vogue* featured Jennifer Lopez, the magazine referenced many of her achievements but let readers know that looking "Insanely Good at 53" was one of them. *Jezebel* was not having it. "I know this may come as a surprise, but it is possible to compliment a middle-aged woman without positioning her as youth-adjacent. We can just say she looks good—not for her age, but for humankind in general," wrote Emily Leibert. In a 2020 *Elle* piece on the launch of her beauty line, JLo Beauty, Lopez talked about her frustration with people telling her she looks good for fifty. "You never want to hear you look great for fifty. They want to just hear you look great, no matter what age you are," she said.

When someone tells me I look good for my age (fifty-two), I cringe. I hate it as much as when I reveal my age and people respond with, "You don't look that old at all!" Thanks, I'm not! Pop culture refuses to let women like Aniston and Lopez age, constantly tying them back to their youth ("16 Ways Jennifer Lopez Makes 51 Look 31," read a *Cosmo* headline), constantly trying to imply their age is imperfect and that youth is the only answer. Let's also stop using the term "anti-aging" like aging is a fate worse than Ben Affleck being without Dunkin' Donuts, and let's stop describing women's skin as "youthful" or "dewy." "Aging is fully in," actress and model Julia Fox said on TikTok, adding, "if I see another product that says anti-aging on the label, I'm suing. I'm going to sue." I never thought I would agree with Fox.

Aniston's *Allure* cover was soon old news, as was her IVF story. A week later, the tabloids were back on the Aniston baby train. "A Baby Girl For Jen!" read the *In Touch* coverline. Apparently, she was "finally adopting at 53." I can't wait for them to ask Hamm what he thinks.

Live Through This:
Courtney Love at Fifty-five

IT'S HARD TO TELL WHETHER Thurston Moore is being sarcastic or sincere. It's probably a bit of both. "The biggest star in this room is Courtney Love," says the Sonic Youth singer and guitarist in a scene from *1991: The Year Punk Broke*. The documentary follows Sonic Youth's summer 1991 European tour and features performances and backstage antics from their tourmates, including a pre-*Nevermind* Nirvana, Babes in Toyland, and Dinosaur Jr.

Moore makes the comment during an interview with *120 Minutes*, an MTV program that spotlighted alternative music in the days before the music channel became the home of teen moms and spoiled Laguna Beach brats. As Moore declares his love of English food to the host—most definitely sarcasm—Love is behind him, trying to get the camera's attention. She waves and appears to stand on something to make herself taller. Her efforts pay off, and soon she is in front of the host, all brazen, blonde, and sporting blue baby doll barrettes.

Tongue-in-cheek or not, Moore was right. Love's band, Hole, wasn't on the European tour bill that summer, and their debut album, *Pretty on the Inside*, hadn't even been released yet, but Love was already on MTV.

Pretty on the Inside was released in the US in September 1991, but it would take me a few months to discover it by fluke, plucking it from a random stack of CDs my friend kept in her car. I chose it because the cover art reminded me of a zine and because I really, really could not listen to Soundgarden's *Badmotorfinger*, my friend's driving soundtrack of choice, one more time. *Pretty on the Inside* was chosen only for temporary relief from "Rusty Cage" on repeat, but instead, it changed my life.

In the 2011 documentary *Hit So Hard*, about the life of Hole drummer Patty Schemel, Love calls *Pretty on the Inside* "unlistenable," but that fall, it was all I would listen to. The album's sound was noisy, confrontational, and messy, and I loved it. It felt abrasive like sandpaper to my twenty-year-old ears. Hearing Love scream and snarl felt cathartic. I worked at a restaurant at the time, and shouting, "*Is she pretty on the inside? Is she pretty from the back?*" along with her made the pain of endless soup, salad, and breadsticks go away. It also made my invites for after-shift drinks with co-workers evaporate. They favoured prim and proper pop princesses and were uncomfortable with the raw, in-your-face lyrics ("*You want her on the bed with her legs wide open and her eyes all spread*") they heard coming from the crappy dish pit speakers. On the plus side, I started getting my orders much faster, since, presumably, the kitchen staff feared I would unleash Courtney-like rage or screams if my pasta primavera took too long.

But it wasn't just Love's screams that intrigued me. Her lyrics were intense and confessional ("*I've seen the things you put me through and I, I wish I could die*"). This was the first time I heard a woman sing about body image, rape, abortion, and self-destruction ("*She tears the hole up even wider / Lets all the darkness up inside her*"). Hole's music was not only groundbreaking; it was honest and real. "I sometimes feel that no one's taken the time to write about certain things in rock," Love said in an interview with *Melody Maker* when the album was released. "There's a certain female point of view that's never been given space."

Pretty on the Inside's first single, "Teenage Whore," would go on to reach number one on the UK indie chart. The album received positive reviews in the *Village Voice*, *The New Yorker,* and *Melody Maker*, among other outlets. It was also named one of the twenty best albums of the year by *Spin*. Writing in *The New Yorker*, Elizabeth Wurtzel described it as "the most compelling album to have been released in 1991," while *Melody Maker*'s Sharon O'Connell called it "the very best bit of fucked up rock 'n' roll" she had heard all year.

The number one song in America the week *Pretty on the Inside* was released was "Promise of a New Day" by Paula Abdul. The future reality show judge's plans for her new day definitely didn't include being a teenage whore, so I sidestepped Paula, and *Pretty on the Inside* became my number one. I also settled into my new part-time job defending Love.

Years later, this job is still on my résumé, and it's not without occupational hazards. I have been in many heated arguments about Love. I have been asked to leave at least one party. In my defence, I already had my coat on. Her name appears as the number one item on several lists made by friends of things we don't discuss because we have moved well beyond an agree-to-disagree truce at this point. I have also had a red Solo cup full of warm gin and tonic thrown at me by a guy who really, really believed Love killed her husband. Not only was he wrong but it was a waste of perfectly lovely top-shelf gin, which really should not be consumed in frat party glassware in the first place.

Not only have I been a lifelong passionate defender of Love but I have also been a believer that if Generation X and the flannel-loving alternative '90s had a hero, it was not, as everyone claims, Kurt Cobain but Courtney Love instead. "She's not supposed to be alive. She's supposed to be a pretty corpse," says Smashing Pumpkins front man Billy Corgan in the 2006 documentary *The Return of Courtney Love.* Love not only lived through the '90s, she clawed her way out from under her husband's shadow and refused to play the widow role everyone wanted and expected her to. She fought critics, conspiracy theorists, and Cobain lovers, stage-diving headfirst into all of them and emerging the ultimate survivor. There is nothing more heroic than that.

Through a combination of resilience, resolve, and reinvention, Love has been a best-selling musician and outspoken front woman, a cultural and feminist icon, a Golden Globe–nominated actress, and an inspiration to girls with guitars everywhere. She subverts the notion of what a female musician should be, how she should look, and how she should act. While male artists are repeatedly celebrated for their ambition, antics, and their addictions, Love is constantly judged for them. Also, a decade that saw the rise of third-wave feminism and a movement like grunge that championed women's rights and power should have a woman for a spokesperson rather than a man. It should be Love, not Cobain.

This July, Love turns fifty-five, an age when we start to think about retirement and taking stock of our lives and our accomplishments. In honour of this milestone birthday, let's celebrate Love's musical, artistic, and cultural impact. Let's finally make Love the girl with the most cake.

This year is important for Love, not only because she turns fifty-five but also because 2019 marks the twenty-fifth anniversary of *Live Through This*, Hole's breakthrough album. Released on April 12, 1994, the critically acclaimed album landed on many "best of the year" lists, including those of the *Village Voice* (number one), *Rolling Stone* (number eight), and *Spin* (number one). Being included among best-selling albums from Pearl Jam, Nirvana, and Soundgarden proved Love could compete with the grunge male heavyweights of the day. *Rolling Stone*'s list of the fifty greatest grunge albums has *Live Through This* at number four, with Hole being the only band featuring a woman (let alone three) in the top ten. A 2016 issue of British music magazine *Q* celebrated the twenty-fifth anniversary of grunge with a list of the twenty-five most influential grunge albums. The list includes *Live Through This* at number twenty-three, the only entry from a band featuring women.

Despite what nostalgia, best-of lists, and the *New York Times* might tell you, '90s alternative culture was not always so progressive and accepting. Success was still largely a male-dominated field, and being angry and angsty was allowed—and even celebrated—if you were Trent or Eddie but not so much if you were Courtney. If you were a lady and wanted to be angsty, they made Lilith Fair for that. "While our culture admires the angry young man, who is perceived as heroic and sexy, it can't find anything but scorn for the angry young woman, who is seen as emasculating and bitter," said Kim France, paraphrasing Susan Faludi in a 1996 *New York Magazine* piece on the new breed of angry women rockers that included PJ Harvey, Liz Phair, and women-fronted bands like Veruca Salt.

For critics who doubted Love's talent and viewed her as nothing more than a gold digger or a groupie, seeing her compete with, and have success alongside, Eddie Vedder, Beck, and Trent Reznor, as well as Cobain, gave her and Hole currency. For me, it provided inspiration and hope. Hole is one of only seven bands featuring women on *Rolling Stone*'s list of the forty best albums of 1994, and I remember how excited I was to see them in the top ten. My excitement was somewhat short lived when I discovered *Rolling Stone* was happy to reward the success of a woman with a tired sexist treatment. The magazine's review spends most of its word count talking about Love's famous husband.

Although regarded as more pop than punk, *Live Through This* is the album that gave us some of the band's best songs, including "Violet" (a personal favourite), "Miss World," the first single from the album, and "Doll Parts." *Live Through This* continued the feminist themes Love first explored in *Pretty on the Inside*, and while she was still angry, her screaming was a little more radio-friendly now.

Despite the mainstream appeal of *Live Through This*, Love remained the punk powerhouse she always was. I remember seeing the video for "Miss World" for the first time on MTV. It features Love as a pageant contestant in her fancy tiara and satin ball gown but singing the very unbeauty queen lyrics "*Somebody kill me, kill me pills.*" Part live performance, Love can be seen aggressively playing her guitar, and at the end of the video, she stage-dives into the crowd, something pop princesses like Mariah Carey definitely weren't doing on MTV at the time (both the diving and the playing of actual instruments).

"That's why a band like Hole was so important, because they were in the mainstream. A figure like Courtney Love and an album like this provided a way into things that were more difficult to access," said Anwen Crawford in an interview about her 33 1/3 book, devoted to *Live Through This*.

The cover art for *Live Through This* shows a photo of a beauty queen complete with a crown and feathered blonde hair but mascara running down her face. Instead of giving a polite, camera-friendly smile, her mouth is wide open (in my mind, she is letting out a "fuck you" to the photographer). Controversies and critics who only see her vulgarity often overshadow the feminist aspects of Love and her work. Throughout her career, she has challenged traditional notions of femininity, and the *Live Through This* cover is a perfect example. Love has taken a conventional symbol of femininity (the beauty queen) and deconstructed it, showing both the beauty and the ugliness of the image. Behind the beauty queen is the pain of what it took her to get there, and her running eye makeup is the crack in her surface as that pain starts to manifest.

In the early '90s, Love and Hole were often lumped in with Bikini Kill's Kathleen Hanna and the riot grrrl scene underway in Olympia, Washington. While *Pretty on the Inside* could easily have been mistaken for a riot grrrl album, the similarities ended there. "Hole had a lot of teenage fans, but Courtney was a good decade older than most of the riot grrrls. The kinds of things she was interested in as a songwriter had a different emphasis, and the things she was interested in as a feminist, too. Courtney was a mess. She was fine with being a mess, and there was no resolution or happy ending for a band like Hole. [The riot grrrls'] music was just as volatile and challenging, but they were ultimately interested in a moral and ethical transformation. Hole was not," said Crawford.

Love has often had an uneasy relationship with the riot grrrl movement. She liked the music but didn't want the politics. "'Don't do it! Sellout!' Girls were throwing riot grrrl zines at me and stuff. I was like 'Uh, I'm really glad you're here, girls, but check it out: I can write a bridge now,'" she told *Rolling Stone* in 1993 of the backlash around Hole's more pop sound.

Riot grrrls didn't want mainstream success, and Love did. When media attention and misconceptions became too much, the riot grrrls declared a media boycott. The only thing harder to imagine than Love boycotting the media is her quitting Twitter. Her lack of desire to align herself with riot grrrl and her lack of an Evergreen College education may be the reason some have trouble seeing her as a feminist, viewing her as more opposition than ally, more brashmobile than bratmobile. "I am a feminist, and I've always thought of myself as a feminist. What I don't like about feminism, and the far left in general, is the infighting, the way that the far left infights too much to get anything done, and I feel like in feminism it's like, 'Well, she's not really feminist enough,' and there can be this kind of less-than thing in feminism," Love said in a 2016 interview for the Liberatum Women in Creativity series.

From her songwriting themes to her influence on young female musicians to how she smashed the stereotypes of how a front woman should act, Love is definitely feminist enough.

Live Through This was supposed to provide Love an opportunity to step out of her famous husband's shadow. "It's annoying now, and it's been annoying for nine years," Love said in a 1999 *Jane* magazine interview of always being connected to Cobain. Released four days after Cobain's body was found, the album's promotion was put on hold. Rather than retreat from the public eye, Love openly mourned and helped fans of Cobain and Nirvana make sense of the singer's death. She sat with grieving teenagers gathered outside the couple's Seattle home and recorded a reading of parts of his suicide note that was played at the singer's memorial that gathered near the Space Needle. In the days following his death, Love showed a very raw and emotional side and admitted that, like many fans, she didn't have all the answers.

It was, and still is, impossible for people to discuss *Live Through This* without noting the irony of the album's title. Love has said the name was not a prediction at all but instead a reflection of all she had endured in the months leading up to its release, including a very public custody fight with the Los Angeles Department of Family Services over daughter Frances Bean. Rumours suggested that Cobain had written much of *Live Through This* (it's Miss World, not Mister, just FYI). "I'd be proud as hell to say that he wrote something on it, but I wouldn't let him. It was too Yoko for me. It's like, 'No fucking way, man! I've got a good band, I don't fucking need your help,'" was Love's response to critics in *Spin*'s oral history of *Live Through This*. Love and Cobain often shared notebooks and lyrics with each other, and while there is talk of Cobain's influence on Love's work, or the writing of all of it, less is mentioned in the press of her impact on his lyrics and music. Rather than suck all the life out of Nirvana or threaten the success of the band, like many assumed she would do, she inspired Cobain. Fun fact: *In Utero*, Nirvana's third album, was named for a line from one of Love's poems.

Songwriting rumours would be replaced by other ones. Women are often vilified and condemned for the deaths of their male partners. Love, like all women, was supposed to save her partner from death and addiction. Fans of Cobain projected all their anger and resentment over the loss of the Nirvana front man onto Love, and soon she was blamed for not only his addiction but also his death. There are even two movies devoted to the theory that Courtney killed Kurt: the awful *Soaked in Bleach* (2015) and the equally awful *Kurt & Courtney* (1998). If you think we've come a long way, baby, sadly we haven't.

One year after Anthony Bourdain's death, Asia Argento is still being blamed, and in September, Ariana Grande had to take a break from social media after fans blamed her for the death of her ex Mac Miller. A few months later, she would be blamed for new beau Pete Davidson's mental health and addiction issues. It's amazing she finds the time to write hit songs, what with all the dude destruction she has going on. When women are not being blamed for the deaths of the men in their lives, they are being attacked for not grieving properly. "She wasn't crying. She's got $30 million coming to her. Do you blame her for being so cool?" a hospital staffer said of Yoko Ono following John Lennon's murder in 1980.

About four months after Cobain's death, Love went on tour to promote her new album. Some questioned and judged why she would go on tour so soon, but Love has said it was a necessity. She had a young daughter to support. She needed to work. She also, sadly, still needed to prove herself. "I would like to think that I'm not getting the sympathy vote, and the only way to do that is to prove that what I've got is real," Love told *Rolling Stone* in 1994. Not only did Cobain's death overshadow the album but it also meant Hole bassist Kristen Pfaff's death two months later received significantly less attention than it should have.

Decades later, Cobain's death still hangs over *Live Through This*. In the days leading up to the anniversary of Cobain's death, former Hole bassist Melissa Auf der Maur wrote an open letter to music magazine *Kerrang*, saying she "would not stand for Kurt's death overshadowing the life and work of the women he left behind this year."

"We were extremely well designed for each other," Love has said of her relationship with Cobain. In a letter reprinted in *Dirty Blonde: The Diaries of Courtney Love*, she calls him "my everything, the top half on my fraction." The two had similar upbringings: both came from broken homes and spent childhoods shuttling between relatives and friends. They both grew up longing for love and acceptance. When we tell the story of Kurt and Courtney, we talk about drugs and destruction, but we don't talk enough about love.

The two also shared an intense drive and ambition. "I didn't want to marry a rock star, I wanted to be one," Love said in a 1992 *Sassy* interview. Evidence of her drive can be found in the many notes and to-do lists she kept, some of which are collected in *Dirty Blonde*. There are reminders to send her acting résumé to agencies, to write three to four new songs a week, to "achieve L.A. visibility." A scene in the documentary *Kurt & Courtney* features an ex of Love's reading from one of her to-do lists, which has "become friends with Michael Stipe" as the number one task to complete (not only did Love do this but he is her daughter's godfather). This ambition is not surprising from a woman who, when she was younger, mailed a tape of herself singing to Neil Sedaka in the hopes of getting signed. Love knew what she wanted at an early age, and what she wanted was fame.

A shrewd businesswoman, her negotiating skills saw *Live Through This* launch the first ever major label bidding war for a female-fronted band, and Hole's seven-album contract earned the band an advance in excess of $1 million and more royalties than Nirvana. She was certainly living by the "Do not hurt yourself, destroy yourself, mangle yourself to *get* the football captain. Be the football captain!" motto she championed in the 1995 documentary *Not Bad for a Girl*. Ambition is often a dirty word when it is used to describe women, and Love is no exception. She has been repeatedly described as calculating and controlling when she should be rewarded for her blonde ambition and viewed as an inspiration. Critics and the press often call her a gold digger who only married Cobain for fame and money. They fail to mention that when the two met, *Pretty on the Inside* was actually selling more copies than *Bleach*, Nirvana's debut album. Even post Kurt, Love's intentions were always under scrutiny. On the *Today Show* to do press for *The People vs. Larry Flynt*, Love refused to talk about her past drug use, despite the host's repeated questions, saying the topic was not an appropriate fit for the show's demographic. She was right, but it didn't stop a writer from describing the move as "calculating" in a 1998 *Spin* piece.

Cobain was ambitious too; he was just much slyer and more secretive about it. He was known to call his manager and complain when MTV didn't play Nirvana's videos enough, and he would correct journalists who misquoted the band's sales figures in interviews. While success is typically celebrated and rewarded for men, and it certainly was for Cobain, he also had to be mindful of the slacker generation that loved Nirvana and greeted success—and especially mainstream success—with *oh, well, whatever, nevermind*.

Love spent two years on the rock stage promoting *Live Through This*, and in 1996, she turned her attention (back) to a different stage. She traded her signature baby doll dresses for ball gowns and transformed herself into a Hollywood movie star. Name-checking musicians was replaced by mentioning famous actor friends and directors she wanted to work with. A *Jane* magazine cover story on Love reveals that "at her first show at the Roseland Ballroom, Courtney drops the names of Cameron Diaz and Matt Dillon. ... During the next five days she goes on to mention Gwyneth Paltrow, Ben Affleck and Drew Barrymore during concerts and TV interviews." Photos from the time show Love hanging out with Barrymore, Winona Ryder, and Kate Moss. Love also traded rock star boyfriends for actor Edward Norton. She became a staple on Hollywood red carpets and best-dressed lists as people talked about her new movie star image. Gone were smeared lipstick and tattered tights, fashion choices that definitely wouldn't appeal to the mainstream movie-going public Love was now courting.

Even though Love's appearance is often judged, her influence on fashion has always been downplayed. In the '90s, her baby doll dresses, barrettes, and Mary Janes were a subversive fashion statement, with the kinderwhore aesthetic being one of the defining styles of the decade. Kinderwhore again saw Love challenging traditional notions of femininity by taking baby doll dresses and knee socks, typically good-girl, childlike elements of fashion and turning them on their barrette-adorned heads. There was Love commanding the stage wearing a Peter Pan collar dress and Mary Janes but singing

"*Go on, take everything, take everything, I want you to.*" In 1994, I worked at a bank and was often written up for unprofessional dressing. When I told the boss it was the kinderwhore look, he told me to dress like a reform school six-year-old on my own time. Fair enough.

Love's cleaned-up image and movie star transformation were called her second act, the age of New Courtney. "It becomes clear that you are in the presence of a new Courtney Love—one who often bears little resemblance to the punk provocateur normally on display," a 1997 *Telegraph* piece proclaimed. Love starred in five films between 1996 and 1999, including *Feeling Minnesota* and *200 Cigarettes*, but her biggest role was playing Althea Flynt in Miloš Forman's *The People vs. Larry Flynt*. Love worked hard to get the part, and the performance earned her Oscar buzz, a Golden Globe nomination, and other accolades. "Love proves she is not a rock star pretending to act, but a true actress," said Roger Ebert in his review.

During the age of New Courtney, Hole developed a more mainstream sound, releasing *Celebrity Skin* in 1998. The band's normally subversive cover art was replaced with a boring generic shot of the four band members with something burning behind them (maybe their punk cred?). The album was dedicated to Los Angeles, fitting given the city is often associated with reinvention, and Love was in the process of her own rebirth. Writing in *The New Yorker* on the twentieth anniversary of the album, Naomi Fry said that the reinvention took "Love from a chaotic, thrift-store-wearing avatar of the grunge era to a kempt, Versace-gown-clad star, and that makeover continued into the studio: in many ways, Hole's third album smoothed the band's difficult, discordant rock into something more commercially palatable." Not only was the singer earning awards for her acting but *Celebrity Skin* earned Hole its first number one single for the album's title track. It topped the year's best-of lists and was nominated for four Grammys.

But critics remained skeptical of Love's transformation and refused to let the old Courtney go. In interviews, she was still asked about drugs, about Cobain's death, and about the tabloid-fodder aspects of her life. Instead of focusing on her acting, a 1995 Barbara Walters interview with Love begins with Walters asking her if she is on heroin. Love's past, misogyny, and the skeptics kept her from ever being fully embraced by Hollywood, meaning she was once again an outsider, just as she had been with the riot grrrls and as the most infamous grunge girl.

Instead of celebrating Love for her reinvention, her second act was always questioned, picked apart, and greeted with distrust. "Once an icon of uncompromising female rage, she now seemed grasping and shallow, hungering for fame and acceptance as a movie star, putting on designer gowns to attend the Academy Awards and posing for Richard Avedon ads for Versace. Was she anything more than just desperately ambitious?" said writer Philip Weiss in a 1998 *Spin* cover story on Love.

Love was not allowed to exist outside the widow,

trainwreck, fucked-up front woman narrative others had created for her. The world would not accept or trust Love as both an actress and a rock star, even though we never question men when they pursue both. Will Smith started the '90s moving in with his auntie and uncle in Bel-Air and ended the decade in the *Wild Wild West*, with two successful albums in between, but there was no way Love was going to start the decade with *Pretty on the Inside* and end it pretty on the outside in Versace.

Love's acting ambitions were described as calculated, even though she had been acting for a long time, including an audition for *The Mickey Mouse Club* under the name Coco Rodriguez when she was young. "I tried out for *The Mickey Mouse Club* when I was eleven. But I read a Sylvia Plath poem about incest, so that wasn't really flying with Disney," she said of her first acting audition. Ten years before *The People vs. Larry Flynt*, Love starred as Gretchen in Alex Cox's *Sid and Nancy* after initially auditioning for the role of Nancy Spungen. Cox was so impressed with Love and her onscreen presence, despite her being in only a handful of scenes in the movie, that he made her the lead in his next film, *Straight to Hell*. These two performances led to Love being a New York celebutante of sorts in the late '80s. She appears in a February 1987 piece in *Interview* magazine and also in a 1987 segment of Andy Warhol's *Fifteen Minutes*, where host Debbie Harry calls Love "a flamboyant rising new star." Her acting career and accolades were not a calculated public relations makeover, as some suspected. Love had, in fact, always been an actress, saying she wanted to act since seeing ten-year-old Tatum O'Neal win the Oscar for *Paper Moon*. She started doing commercials and youth theatre, telling the *LA Times*, "I owned the Pacific Northwest when it came to the children's slot in radio jingles and voice-overs."

What she hadn't wanted to be was a tabloid headline. Drama and dysfunction have often obscured Love's talent and accomplishments. She was the original tabloid target: her legal troubles and addiction issues coincided with the rise of tabloid journalism, the birth of *TMZ*, and the popularity of celebrity gossip blogs. Love was the first female star of the '90s to have her personal life judged and picked apart and her self-destruction be a regular part of the around-the-clock news cycle. This set the tone for how tabloids cover the lives and exploits of so-called troubled female celebrities, from Lindsay Lohan to Amy Winehouse to Britney Spears. Their work, talent, and art are always overshadowed by coverage that focuses on drugs, mental health issues, and arrests, or they are reduced to punchlines.

While female celebrities like Love are criticized for their rebellion, male celebrities, like Cobain, for example, are celebrated and mythologized for it. Cobain and Love both struggled with addiction, but it is Love who is repeatedly vilified for her drug use. "She was vilified for being a mess, for being a drug addict, for not being a great parent—in other words, all of the things we expect in a male rock star," said *Bust* in a piece in the magazine's twentieth anniversary issue, which featured Love on the cover.

We make jokes about the drug antics of male celebrities, from Keith Richards to Charlie Sheen, idolizing their debauchery and depravity. The new Netflix/Lifetime movie *The Dirt*, about Mötley Crüe, takes the band's excesses to almost comic levels. Check out crazy tourmate Ozzy Osbourne snorting a line of ants by a hotel pool! Such zany antics! I would love to see Lindsay Lohan try to get away with that. We never allow women to live down their arrests and their addictions, but we repeatedly allow men to have a redemption arc. Robert Downey Jr. was in and out of jail and on and off drugs for much of the mid to late '90s, but we rarely, if ever, talk about his past.

When Love isn't being attacked for her addiction issues, she is being judged for her parenting. Her first instance of unflattering press was "Strange Love," the much publicized 1992 *Vanity Fair* profile by Lynn Hirschberg. While the piece talks at length about Love's drug use and constantly questions her parenting ability, it doesn't paint Cobain in the same light. "It is appalling to think that she would be taking drugs when she knew she was pregnant," says one close friend in the piece. Hirschberg relies on many unnamed sources and focuses often on the tabloid-like aspects of Love's life and addictions. "Courtney has a long history with drugs. She loves Percodans ('They make me vacuum'), and has dabbled with heroin off and on since she was eighteen, once even snorting it in Room 101 of the Chelsea Hotel, where Nancy Spungen died," she writes. "Reportedly, Kurt didn't do much more than drink until he met Courtney."

This double standard was common in coverage of the couple. In *Kurt Cobain: Montage of Heck*, the 2015 documentary by Brett Morgen, Love asks her husband, "Why does everyone think you're the good one and I'm the bad one?" Later in the film, we see a scene of Frances Bean's first haircut. The child sits in Cobain's lap while Love searches for a comb and scissors. The camera shows Cobain nodding off, and while he maintains that he is just tired, it's clear he's not. The scene is painful to watch, especially because those around Cobain carry on like nothing is wrong, giving the feeling this is just like any other day in the Love-Cobain household. The scene is a reminder of how the press treated Cobain's addiction when he was alive. They just carried on like nothing was wrong, instead directing all their judgment at Love.

This year, Love's first solo album, *America's Sweetheart*, turns fifteen. Released on February 10, 2004, it was a disappointment for Love, selling fewer than 100,000 copies and receiving mostly negative reviews. In 2010, she released *Nobody's Daughter*, with a revamped Hole, which was greeted with mixed reviews. She has also branched out from music over the past few years, and her influence on pop culture shows no signs of letting up. She released her diaries in book form as *Dirty*

Blonde in 2006, mounted an art show called *And She's Not Even Pretty*, collaborated on a fashion line called Never the Bride, became the face of Yves St. Laurent, has been a judge on *RuPaul's Drag Race*, and co-wrote a manga series. She has a bit part in the film *JT LeRoy* and has appeared on television, with roles on *Empire*, *Sons of Anarchy*, and as Kitty Menendez in the Lifetime movie devoted to the murders by the Menendez brothers.

Each time Love stars on a television show, appears in a movie, or releases a new album, headlines proclaim her "return," even though she has never gone anywhere. It is as if the media and critics want her to prove herself all over again. When men retreat from the spotlight or take a break from making art, there is no comeback narrative. Even if the media does declare a "new Courtney Love," in my mind, they still never let Love escape the old Courtney. They are always skeptical, always distrusting, always assuming she is on drugs. They will never really let Love have her second (or third or fourth) act. As I write this, there's news that Mel Gibson—who is antisemitic, homophobic, abusive to women, and once called a female police officer "sugar tits" after being pulled over for DUI—has been cast in a new movie. Called *Rothchild*, the movie also stars Shia LaBeouf, who has had his own issues with arrests and alcohol. I originally thought this casting announcement was an *Onion* story. I can't wait for the new buddy movie starring Lindsay Lohan and Courtney Love. Maybe they can do a remake of *Weekend at Bernie's*, and the corpse can be played by the careers of both female stars.

Hole was one of the most popular and successful female-fronted bands of the '90s, and when we discuss Love's cultural impact, we can't underestimate the influence she has had on female musicians, this author included. "I want every girl in the world to pick up a guitar and start screaming," she said in a 1996 interview. She has been name-checked for her role in inspiring young female musicians, from Alanis Morissette to Lana Del Rey.

"I saw Courtney Love playing guitar on MTV in the 'Doll Parts' video and I immediately was like, 'I can do that.' I hadn't seen any other women on TV making music before, so I didn't even realize it was possible," said War on Women front woman Shawna Potter in a 2017 *New York Times* piece on rock being ruled by women (apparently a new thing).

Love has always been a great front woman, although she prefers to be called a front man, rebelling against the idea of how a woman on stage should act. She is not afraid to take up space. As in life, she is outspoken, she is unpredictable, she is messy, and she is raw. She will not stand politely before you, quietly strumming her guitar, or do a choreographed dance dressed like a giant cupcake, even though I would pay very good money to see that. If she did, the icing would probably be running down her face like the mascara on the *Live Through This* cover. Male musicians are allowed, and expected, to wail and scream on stage, and Love has always showed that she could give as good as her male counterparts.

Her live shows are often unpredictable, but the spectacle should never replace the song. When I saw Love in Toronto in 2013, the people beside me complained throughout the show, and at an unacceptable volume, that Love didn't throw a microphone stand into the crowd or verbally assault the entire front row. It's too bad that their complaining made them miss a great performance. One of them was wearing a Cobain shirt, which deserves a verbal assault.

When Soundgarden's Chris Cornell died in 2017, articles mourned the loss and talked about how Eddie Vedder of Pearl Jam was the last grunge hero standing. Love deserves the title much more than Vedder—for all she has endured, for her strength, and for her musical and film contributions. Male musicians can write "pro-choice" on their arms with felt markers all they want, but grunge has never fully acknowledged or accepted the contributions of women and female musicians, so the Vedder pronouncement was no surprise.

Love has always been an outsider, whether it be from her family, from the male-dominated Seattle scene, from riot grrrls, or from Hollywood. But it is this status that makes Love the ultimate spokesperson for a generation that wanted to exist in the margins. With a career that has spanned decades, she is a survivor, despite all of those who bet on her self-destruction. If we acknowledge that the alternative movement of the '90s began when *Pretty on the Inside* was released and was wrapped up by the time *Celebrity Skin* was replaced by boy bands and Britney, then Love was not only the girl with the most cake but also the last one standing.

Her birthday aside, this year seems like the perfect time to celebrate Love. The girl culture of the '90s is back. Bikini Kill is on tour this year and playing to sold-out crowds. The *New York Times* recently published a piece asking the question "What was, or is, riot grrrl? A movement, a genre, an era, a scene?" *Her Smell*, a movie starring Elisabeth Moss as a very thinly veiled Courtney Love, is in theatres, and new memoirs from Ani DiFranco and Liz Phair are being released this year.

So, on her fifty-fifth birthday, may Love be what she always has been and always should be: the girl with the most cake. Happy birthday, Courtney.

Amy Deserves Better

"Please don't touch the display, miss." The security guard had already warned me twice, so I snapped some pictures and quickly moved on. Inside the display's glass was the drum kit Dave Grohl played in Nirvana's third album, *In Utero*. It was part of the *Nirvana: Taking Punk to the Masses* exhibit at Seattle's Museum of Pop Culture—which was the reason I was visiting on an unusually sunny Saturday afternoon in March 2013. My fear of flying means I travel only if there is something I really want to see, like my mom, or the sweater Kurt Cobain wore in the "Smells Like Teen Spirit" video. I visited the exhibit multiple times while I was in Seattle, along with the other destinations on the "grunge vacation highlights" spreadsheet I carefully researched and compiled before my trip.

On my last day in Seattle, I still had one big item left on my sightseeing agenda: the house where Cobain died in 1994. The idea of visiting the spot made me uncomfortable because of the morbidity attached to it, but like many other Nirvana fans, I was also curious. In the end, I decided I would regret not seeing it, so I mapped my route to 171 Lake Washington Boulevard East and, because I am a total cliché, listened to *In Utero* on the walk from my hotel.

The house Cobain died in sits on a hill in Seattle's posh Denny-Blaine neighbourhood and overlooks Lake Washington. He lived there only for three months, with wife Courtney Love and their daughter, Frances Bean Cobain, purchasing it for $1.48 million in January 1994. Some fans labelled Cobain a sellout for living in a four-bedroom, five-bathroom house in a wealthy neighbour-hood where his neighbours included Starbucks CEOs and tech bigwigs. He famously sang, "Teenage angst has paid off well," and judging from his house, it certainly had. Fans who felt betrayed that the "crown prince of Gen X" was living large would have preferred he still lived under that bridge in his hometown of Aberdeen, Washington. Whether he actually lived there is a matter of debate, but it's part of the mythology the singer told reporters and immortalized in songs like "Something in the Way."

The house looked smaller than I remembered, having seen pictures of it on the front pages of newspapers and accompanied by Kurt Loder voiceovers on MTV following Cobain's death in April 1994. Beside the house is Viretta Park, which was turned into an informal Cobain memorial park. When I visited, the space was mostly grass, a few trees, and a wooden park bench covered in Cobain-related graffiti, my favourite scrawl being "Hole Was Better." There were a few people milling around: a couple taking pictures of the house, two German tourists reading the bench graffiti, and some young guys from Japan who parked their rented Volvo in front of the park, rolled down the windows, and played Nirvana's cover of "The Man Who Sold the World" on repeat. We made small talk about what a great songwriter Cobain was, which I found ironic since they were blasting a song Cobain didn't actually write.

I have thought about that afternoon in Seattle many times over the years. I remembered spending hours camped out in front of the television in the days after Cobain's death, afraid to leave the room to use the washroom or get a glass of water, for fear of missing a detail. I waited for magazines to arrive on newsstands and collected them all, from *People* to *NME* to *Rolling Stone*. Friends joined me in front of the television. We read each other stories about Cobain from the newspaper and rolled our eyes whenever newscaster Dan Rather attempted to explain "the Seattle sound" to us.

Amy Winehouse was also on my mind a lot during my Seattle visit. The British singer died on July 23, 2011, of alcohol poisoning, at the age of twenty-seven. Social media and the internet announced the news twenty minutes after her body was found. It would be another forty before news channels broke the story. Winehouse soon became a trending topic, and I remember googling her name to get confirmation. It's an all-too-familiar pattern now. A celebrity trends, and we fear the worst. Dying in the age of clickbait meant that the headlines highlighted Winehouse's cause of death. "Too much alcohol," said the *New York Post*, while others frequently referenced her "downward spiral" and the singer's "tragic death."

It's hard to avoid drawing comparisons between Winehouse and Cobain. "The interplay between Ms. Winehouse's life and art made her one of the most fascinating figures in pop music since Kurt Cobain, whose demise in 1994—also at age 27—was preceded by drug abuse and a frustration with fame as something that could never be escaped," wrote Ben Sisario in the *New York Times*. They both shared the childhood trauma of divorce, subject matter that found its way into their songs and which they frequently downplayed when reporters psychoanalyzed their lyrics. "Grunge is what happens when children of divorce get their hands on guitars," *Newsweek* said of Cobain's music. The singer frequently addressed his frustration with talking about his childhood in interviews and his lyrics. "That legendary divorce is such a bore," he sang in "Serve the Servants."

Both Winehouse and Cobain had a complicated relationship with fame, resenting their success once the whole machine got too big. The singers didn't want all the fancy things their hit songs and sold-out shows afforded: they just wanted to play music. "My music is not on that scale. Sometimes I wish it was, but I don't think I am going to be at all famous. I don't think I could handle it. I'd probably go mad," Winehouse says, in the 2015 documentary *Amy*, of her pre–*Back to Black* status, describing fame as a "scary thing."

They both also altered the course of music and pop

culture, although Cobain is much more acknowledged for his contributions. They used drugs and embraced what others viewed as dysfunctional relationships that were often blamed for their downfalls. Cobain and Winehouse died too soon and from tragic situations, joining the 27 Club of famous musicians and artists whose lives ended at the same age—a club whose membership includes Jimi Hendrix, Jim Morrison, Jean-Michel Basquiat, and Janis Joplin, although the male members are remembered far more often. "Why is she not remembered, talked about as much as any guy who died by himself in a motel? She was left behind as quickly as they could," singer-songwriter Rickie Lee Jones said of Joplin in the 2022 docuseries *Women Who Rock*.

While I appreciate the similarities between Winehouse and Cobain, they end when I think about how the two are remembered and how we talk about what killed them. Addiction comes up frequently in the context of Cobain, both when he was alive and after his death, but he was treated as a passive participant in his drug use. Excuses were made for why he took drugs. He used heroin because of the pressures of fame, because of stomach problems, because he hated his bandmates and the music industry. In contrast, Winehouse was vilified, blamed, and mocked for her addiction, and this treatment continues twelve years after her death. We turned Winehouse into a spectacle and then were shocked when she died.

"The tortured genius, the hellion libertine, the martyr

dying for the noble cause of nihilism—this is what we usually mean when we say 'rock star,' and we're always on the hunt for fresh blood," wrote Steve Kandell in a *Spin* magazine piece days after Winehouse's death. How we treat that fresh blood varies, with the tortured genius being a very gendered concept. In life and in death, Cobain was the voice of a generation, a slacker idol whose contributions remain celebrated. Winehouse, throughout her life and beyond, was a mess: a paparazzi target whose struggles were portrayed as bigger than her trademark beehive and always overshadowed her talent.

Winehouse's sophomore album *Back to Black* was released in October 2006. It followed *Frank*, her critically acclaimed 2003 debut which sold 1 million copies in the UK, was nominated for two Brit Awards, and shortlisted for the Mercury Music Prize. *Back to Black* was not only the best-selling UK album of 2007, with sales of over 1.85 million copies, but also one of the best-selling albums in UK history, sandwiched between Fleetwood Mac's *Rumours* and Adele's *25*. The album's lead single, "Rehab," went to number seven on the UK singles chart and number nine on the Billboard Hot 100 in the US. It was named the best song of 2007 by *Time* magazine and was number seven on *Rolling Stone*'s 100 Best Songs of 2007.

At the 2007 Brit Awards in February, Winehouse took home the British Female Solo Artist award and was nominated for Album of the Year. While she may have won big at the Brits, later that year, the media focused on cancelled tour dates amidst rumours that Winehouse was drunk and couldn't play shows. Bookies started to take bets on whether she would show up for concerts and be able to perform. A few months later, a clip from a video of the singer smoking crack was broadcast by the tabloid *The Sun*.

A year after the Brit Awards, the fiftieth Grammy Awards were held in Los Angeles. Winehouse was still waiting for a visa, so she performed from a stage in London. She became the first British woman to win five Grammys, including Record of the Year, Song of the Year, Best Female Pop Vocal Performance, Best Pop Vocal Album, and Best New Artist. While I have often compared Winehouse to Cobain, there's no contest when it comes to Grammy awards. Nirvana has one Grammy for Best Alternative Music Performance for *MTV Unplugged in New York*. Cobain's suicide also took home "Bummer of the Year" at the 1995 *NME* Awards. Bummer, indeed.

"[A] perfect storm of sex kitten, raw talent and poor impulse control" is how *Newsweek* described Winehouse in a March 2007 piece later saying she is "as well-known for her sharp tongue and alcohol-fueled antics as she is for her emotive soul music." When she died, the *Washington Post* commented that "the more Amy Winehouse drinks, the better she sings," which was not an opinion everyone shared. While Winehouse won big at the fiftieth Grammy Awards, there was one award she didn't receive: Album of the Year. *Back to Black* was nominated but lost to *River:*

The Joni Letters by Herbie Hancock, an album that was not only a covers album but sold significantly fewer copies than *Back to Black*. "Evidently, the most conservative voters—and there are a lot of them—got too distracted by her image problems to see that she created a classic," said *Entertainment Weekly* music critic Chris Willman of Winehouse's Album of the Year loss.

Her "image problems" were definitely the topic of post-Grammys conversation. Singer Natalie Cole, who, along with Tony Bennett, presented the Record of the Year Grammy to Winehouse, questioned whether she should have won given her drug and alcohol problems. "We have to stop rewarding bad behaviour. I'm sorry. I think the girl is talented, gifted, but it's not right for her to be able to have her cake and eat it too. She needs to get herself together," said Cole. "I don't think anybody wanted to be giving awards to somebody for a song about not wanting to go to rehab," said *Rolling Stone* contributing editor Anthony DeCurtis, adding, "that's only funny if you don't have to go."

Winehouse entered a rehab facility prior to the Grammys, but that shouldn't have mattered, and her wins would not have been such a hot topic if she were a man. CNN was outraged and asked whether Winehouse should have been banned from the Grammys. *Showbiz Tonight* wondered if Winehouse was just "another star being rewarded for bad behaviour." I thought about this outrage when the 2022 Grammy nominations were announced. The list included a homophobic comedian (Kevin Hart), a transphobic comedian (David Chappelle), an abusive comedian (Louis C.K.), and an abusive musician (Marilyn Manson). At the time, Recording Academy CEO Harvey Mason Jr. said, "We won't restrict the people who can submit their material for consideration. We won't look back at people's history, we won't look at their criminal record, we won't look at anything other than the legality within our rules of, is this recording for this work eligible based on date and other criteria." Louis C.K. went on to win Best Comedy Album at the 2022 Grammys. Chappelle took the honours in 2023.

Even the United Nations weighed in on Winehouse's addiction issues. In a newspaper piece, UN Office of Drugs and Crime executive director Antonio Maria Costa talked about how Winehouse and her drug use set a bad example for others struggling with addiction and also undermined the work of celebrities attempting to raise awareness of the problems in Africa, a continent tied to the UK's cocaine supply. Winehouse's representative, rightfully, told the UN to stay in its lane. The Grammys controversy may not have been good for Winehouse, but it helped sell records. Post-awards *Back to Black* went from number twenty-four to number two on the Billboard 200 chart. Consuming Winehouse's pain was fine but awarding her for it, well, not so much.

"This past year, Amy Winehouse, 24, has gone from being one of pop music's most ascendant and celebrated talents to a tragicomic train wreck of epic proportions."

That's how the singer is described in a 2008 *Rolling Stone* cover story by Claire Hoffman. The cover featured a picture of Winehouse and the headline "Up All Night With Amy." *Rolling Stone* really distinguished itself with its headlines for Winehouse. Here are a few:

The Diva and Her Demons

Up All Night With Amy Winehouse

Amy Winehouse's Death: A Troubled Star Gone Too Soon

The Tumultuous Life of Amy Winehouse

We get it, *Rolling Stone*. But it's unfair to single out the publication. Its coverage was similar to the majority of the stories about Winehouse. They referenced tabloid tales and were accompanied by photos of a dishevelled and drunk Winehouse roaming the streets in blood-stained ballet slippers. Reporters talked about drugs, romantic affairs, and run-ins with the police. Jokes were made about her self-harm, bulimia, and addiction.

It wasn't just the press that joked about Winehouse. Internet trolls and late-night comedians also mocked her. On a 2006 episode of *Never Mind the Buzzcocks*, a British game show, the host joked of Winehouse, "This isn't even a pop quiz show, it's an intervention." A joke by comedian Zoe Lyons about Winehouse's self-harm was publicly voted funniest joke at the 2008 Edinburgh Fringe. Three months after Winehouse's death, actor Neil Patrick Harris displayed a meat platter called "The Corpse of Amy Winehouse" at his Halloween party buffet. Apparently, Harris thought recreating a gory-looking Winehouse out of chicken sausage and pulled pork, complete with a cigarette hanging out of her mouth, was hilarious. A corpse of meat is gross enough, but specifically making it Winehouse, and labelling it as such, is next level misogyny.

While every detail of Winehouse's addiction was obsessively chronicled and consumed, Cobain's addiction was less documented. Some of this difference can be attributed to the fact that Cobain rose to fame in the pre–social media, pre-*TMZ* days when it was easier to believe the narrative he was pushing, but not all of it can. Cobain often dismissed his addiction, and he frequently changed stories and timelines to suit his interests. Journalists believed Cobain's fiction and covered for him, often because they feared they would lose access to Nirvana and its singer but also out of respect and admiration for the male singer. "He's been suffering from a long-standing and painful stomach condition—perhaps probably an ulcer—aggravated by stress and, apparently, his screaming singing style," read a 1992 *Rolling Stone* cover story on Nirvana. "I walked up to him. He was glad to see me and said that he liked my *Rolling Stone* story," wrote Michael Azerrad in a 2021 *New Yorker* piece on his friendship with Cobain. "In retrospect, I can see why: the article served his purposes.

I quoted an anti-drug speech he gave—which he seemed to think let him off the hook for using drugs."

This was a common story angle in the '90s. Cobain wasn't using drugs: he was just sick with something. When his heroin use was exposed, it was justified because it was said to make his crippling stomach pain better. But the drug rumours increased as Nirvana's fame rose. Music magazine *Hits* published an item about Cobain "slam dancing with Mr. Brownstone," which was code for heroin. Later, a profile in *BAM* mentioned that Cobain was "nodding off" and noted that his "pinned pupils, sunken cheeks and scabbed, sallow skin suggest something more serious than mere fatigue."

At times, Cobain denied drug use saying he didn't even touch alcohol because of his stomach. "My body wouldn't allow me to take drugs if I wanted to, because I'm so weak all the time." Journalists were more than happy to promote his version of events, even when the signs continued, including the nodding off in *Spin* magazine cover shoots and interviews. He called drugs "a waste of time" and spun tales about how he didn't use them or had previously used them for a short time but then quit.

"Last year, Cobain also made a clean break of his long-rumored heroin addiction, claiming he'd used the drug—at least in part—to opiate severe, chronic stomach pain. Or as he puts it in this interview, 'to medicate myself.' He's now off the junk, and thanks to new medication and a better diet, his digestive tract, he says, is on the road to recovery," read a 1994 *Rolling Stone* interview.

After his death, media continued to gloss over Cobain's addiction issues and depression. In her April 1994 *Spin* cover story, writer Gina Arnold talked about Cobain's mythologization. "The fact, for example, that Cobain was clinically depressed—a fact that is self-evident from his actions, and a condition that ran in his family (two of his uncles also committed suicide)—has been overlooked in favor of stories about his symbolic importance." The *LA Times* remembered him as "a reluctant hero who spoke to his generation." Drugs don't come up until the eighth paragraph of the piece. When Winehouse died, the paper wrote, "Amy Winehouse dies at 27; iconoclastic British singer-songwriter." The photo caption described the singer as "troubled," and drugs came up in the fourth paragraph, with comparisons to other male members of the 27 Club popping up in the second. The *New York Times* referred to Cobain as "the hesitant poet of 'Grunge Rock,'" Winehouse? "British Soul Singer With a Troubled Life."

When Nirvana's groundbreaking album *Nevermind* was released by Geffen on September 24, 1991, the label's president, Ed Rosenblatt, called it "one of those 'get out of the way and duck' records." The album's impact has been documented widely, from how it killed hair metal music to how it put the Pacific Northwest on the map and how it voiced the dissatisfaction of an entire generation. To date, it has sold 30 million copies, making it one of the best-selling albums of all time, and in 2021, "Smells Like Teen Spirit" surpassed 1 billion streams on Spotify.

I wish we talked more about Winehouse's impact on music and female musicians, specifically how her success made it easier for unconventional women to achieve success: women who had their own voice and style and didn't fit the traditional pop music mould. Following *Back to Black*, record companies signed Adele, Duffy, Lily Allen, and Florence and The Machine—unconventional female artists who all found success. "Amy Winehouse was the Nirvana moment for all these women," said *Spin*'s music editor, Charles Aaron. "They can all be traced back to her in terms of attitude, musical styles or fashion." Instead, the *LA Times* obit helped set the tone about how she's remembered today, noting her "gaunt and ill-kempt" appearances, her "run-ins with the police, missed or aborted shows and struggles with addictions," and her stay in a London clinic specialized in "treating psychiatric, drug and alcohol problems."

Pieces on Cobain's death often searched for answers, trying to make sense of why the singer took his own life, even though there was no shortage of clues in interviews and song lyrics. Even twenty-nine years after Cobain's death, the fascination with his last days continues. Timelines, books, and movies—both fictional and not so fictional—attempt to explain the singer's motivations. The movies range from the respectful—like Gus Van Sant's 2005 *Last Days*, which the director claims is definitely not about Cobain (wink, wink)—to the tabloidesque *Soaked in Bleach*, told from the perspective of Tom Grant, a private investigator hired by Love to search for Cobain after he jumped the wall at Exodus treatment centre a few days before his death.

With Winehouse, there was little tracing of her final days. Instead, we seemed to be counting down to her inevitable fate. The conspiracy theories around Cobain's death prove people don't want to believe their idol killed himself: they don't want to admit it or take him down from their flannel-covered altar to see him for what he was—which was a flawed and messed-up human who also happened to write really good songs. Acknowledging his flaws doesn't discredit his talent. For Winehouse, the flaws long ago outweighed the talent.

One of the best films about Cobain is 2015's *Kurt Cobain: Montage of Heck*, directed by Brett Morgen, who was given access to the singer's archives and previously unseen material. The film was also made with the blessings and support of Courtney Love and Frances Bean Cobain. "It was time to examine this person and humanize him and decanonize these values that he allegedly stood for— the lack of ambition and these ridiculous myths that had been built up around him," Love told the *New York Times*.

"He's larger than life and our culture is obsessed with dead musicians," said Frances Bean Cobain in *Rolling Stone*. Like her mother, she wanted Morgen's documentary to chip away at the romanticism associated with her father. The film dispels the myth that Cobain was a slacker who didn't want fame, showing notebooks with lists of labels demos were sent to, to-do lists, and numbers for bookers and venues. The movie shows his sense of humour and love for his wife and daughter and also shatters the long-held belief that Love got him hooked on drugs. Oh, and, spoiler alert, he wasn't actually from Seattle.

"Even though both deaths were motivated by depression underscored by narcotics and celebrity," wrote Molly Beauchemin in a 2015 *Pitchfork* essay about Cobain and Winehouse, "*Montage* depicts a context in which the public was willing Cobain to succeed, whereas Winehouse, when confronted with similar drug-addled obstacles, was met with ridicule and slander."

In January 2023, it was announced that a new movie about Winehouse's life, *Back to Black*, was in the works. (The movie is scheduled to be released in 2024, which also marks the thirtieth anniversary of Cobain's death.) When photos from the set were released, social media immediately said no, no, no. Tweets called for people to boycott the film or bluntly said, "This is fucking revolting." Actress Marisa Abela plays Winehouse, and scenes show her dishevelled and distraught, with tears and smudged eye makeup. In other words, they show a talented woman, reduced to a caricature, whose struggles will once again be available for us to consume.

Money Shots

DURING THE SUMMER of 2004, I sat through *Garden State* more times than I will ever admit. In his writing and directorial debut, Zach Braff plays a struggling actor dealing with mental health issues who returns to his hometown for his mom's funeral. Sometimes, when the film ended, I would sneak back into the dark, air-conditioned movie theatre to watch the movie again.

I wasn't blown away by Braff's cinematic genius, nor was the film too complex for me to grasp in one viewing. The truth is the film's release coincided with a period of deep depression. I felt numb, and watching Braff's character deal with his own numbness made me feel less alone. "This is not a perfect movie," Roger Ebert wrote in his review. "It meanders and ambles and makes puzzling detours." He might also have been describing my mental state that summer.

I found some comfort in the film, but I'd also grown up at a time when mental health representations in pop culture were either invisible or one dimensional. Words like "crazy" and "nuts" were widely used, and depictions were played for laughs or linked mental illness with creative weirdos. Depression was a bathrobed person shuffling around until they retreated to bed, where they stared blankly at a wall. Sometimes they had a tiny cartoon storm cloud over their head.

The first time I experienced depression and anxiety, I was in my twenties. It was the '90s, and *Prozac Nation* taught me that mental illness looked like a thin, pretty white girl in vintage Levi's 501s and silver hoop earrings or Winona Ryder in a manic pixie cut in *Girl, Interrupted* or the blonde Lisbon sisters in *Virgin Suicides*. Kurt Cobain talked about depression in interviews, which made it seem cool and subversive, like knowing who the Meat Puppets were or being really into Sonic Youth. In my mid-thirties, when I was finally ready to open up about my situation, a photograph stopped me.

November 28, 2006, is an important milestone in pop culture history. It's the date paparazzi captured the infamous photo of Britney Spears, Lindsay Lohan, and Paris Hilton in the front seat of a car outside the Beverly Hills Hotel during a night out partying. There are various versions of how the photo came to be. Some say it was set up for reporters; others (namely, Hilton) say that she and Spears were leaving the hotel when Lohan, then feuding with Hilton, jumped in the car at the last minute, aware of the impact the image would have.

Whichever story is true, this photo of the Holy Trinity of Celebrity Gossip increased *Us Weekly* sales and Perez Hilton page views for weeks after it was snapped. The *New York Post* dubbed the image the "Bimbo Summit" and quoted a *Newsweek* poll that said 77 percent of adults believed Lohan, Spears, and Hilton had too much influence on the younger generation. Indeed, the trio represented an era of famous starlets that included Nicole Richie, Hilary Duff, Mischa Barton, Tara Reid, Mary-Kate and Ashley Olsen, and Ashlee and Jessica Simpson. Their frenemy feuds, post-nightclub stumbles, mugshots, and meltdowns were obsessively documented. It was the decade of flip phones and Juicy Couture tracksuits and fire crotch, and thanks to the rise of the internet, we had a front-row seat to it all.

Like others, I couldn't get enough of these women. But I began feeling guilty for contributing to a system that was tearing them down, turning their public struggles with mental health and addiction into jokes for late-night TV and exploiting them for newsstand sales. Pop culture's lack of compassion and sensitivity made me too scared to talk about my own issues. Even though my mental health was wreaking more havoc on my life than these young women were on the LA county justice system, I stayed silent.

"Help Me." That was the cover line on the March 5, 2007, issue of *Us Weekly*, which featured a picture of Spears shaving her head. A month earlier, she had entered Esther's Haircutting Studio in Tarzana, California, and asked the owner to shave her head. When Esther Tognozzi refused, Spears picked up the clippers and did it herself. (Fans still visit the salon to see the chair Spears sat in and, while Tognozzi claims to hate the publicity, she still has Spears's hair.)

In the *Us Weekly* cover story, ex-staffers and insiders revealed "Brit's loneliness, self-hatred & drug use." That same week, *People* offered to take readers "Inside Britney's Breakdown," which included "wild partying" and "sobbing in public." *New York Daily News* ran with the headline "Britney Shears: Shocking pix as superstar teeters on edge of a breakdown." It was only slightly less offensive than their "Unfitney" cover story about her losing the custody of her children.

The previous year had been a rough one for Spears. In February 2006, she was photographed driving while holding her young son, Sean, in her lap, leading to speculation about the singer's parenting abilities. A week later, she was photographed almost dropping her son, which again raised concerns. In both instances, Spears blamed paparazzi for recklessly pursuing her and her children. In an NBC *Dateline* interview, Spears broke down and begged the press to leave her alone. In November 2006, only months after the couple's second son was born, she filed for divorce from husband Kevin Federline. In February 2007, she entered rehab in Antigua for less than a day. A few weeks following her head shaving, Spears attacked a paparazzo's car with an umbrella after being swarmed by photographers at a gas station. The singer was in the middle of a custody battle with Federline and had been trying to see her sons that night. The paparazzo would later auction off the umbrella.

The "Help Me" cover line was not *Us Weekly*'s lowest point when it came to Spears. In November 2007, the tabloid ran a cover of Spears with the headline "Sick!" And in January 2008, the magazine called her a "Time Bomb." Jen Peros, a former *Us Weekly* editor, told the *New York Times* in 2021 that Spears's struggles were a boon to print magazines desperate to keep the celebrity gossip mill running. "[W]hen you found a celebrity—I hate to say it—spiraling or acting abnormally, that was the story," Peros explained. "And we knew it would sell magazines."

In February 2008, *Rolling Stone*'s much-hyped exposé on the star declared Spears's as "the most public downfall of any star in history." The story was heartbreaking to read and described Spears not sleeping for days because she feared her thoughts were being recorded by her cellphone charger. Her pain also went mainstream. You could buy a bald Britney Spears Halloween costume online, and contestants on an episode of *Family Feud* were asked to list the things Spears had lost in the past year. Correct answers included "her hair" and "her mind." A Florida morning show host was threatened with legal action after using a photo of a bald Spears with the line "total nut jobs" to promote his morning show on billboards, and "If Britney can survive 2007, you can make it through this" became a popular meme.

In *Framing Britney Spears*, the 2021 documentary about her, a paparazzo called shots of the singer having a meltdown a "money shot." In 2008, the Poynter Institute published the results of a *Portfolio* magazine examination of how much revenue the pop princess generated for magazines. From January 2006 to July 2007, she was on the cover of *People, Us Weekly, In Touch, Life & Style, OK!* and *Star* 175 times in seventy-eight weeks, accounting for $360 million in sales. A Spears cover story could sell 1.28 million copies, almost 33 percent more than a cover not featuring the singer. From 2001 to 2007, Yahoo search rankings placed Spears in the top spot for six of those years. In 2004, she dropped to number two when Hilton took the number one spot. In 2007, the searches for Spears increased 60 percent.

The spectacle was one we all consumed. When *Us Weekly*'s "Sick!" cover appeared, Spears was twenty-five. I was ten years older and remember buying the issue. I didn't immediately read it and instead left it unopened for weeks. I couldn't bring myself to treat Spears's breakdown like it had the same entertainment value as an MTV performance. I finally threw the magazine in my recycling bin.

The pop culture I experienced growing up was no better at depictions of addiction than it was at depictions of mental health. Remember the "This is your brain on drugs" PSAs that compared the effects of drugs to an egg frying in a cast-iron skillet? It mostly just made me crave breakfast foods.

Two celebrity deaths made me think more deeply about how pop culture treated drug use. The first was that of actor River Phoenix, who died outside the Los Angeles nightclub The Viper Room on Halloween 1993. I was, and remain, a huge Phoenix fan, but in an age without internet and social media, his drug use had largely been hidden from the press and his fans. He was a vegan who loved animals and supported PETA. None of these details fit the profile of what we were taught to expect from an addict. The second death was Kurt Cobain's, in 1994. While the press talked about his heroin addiction, it was largely dismissed, or excused, as something used to cope with fame, fans, and media. He had stomach problems; heroin helped. He was sad; heroin helped.

Years after Phoenix's and Cobain's deaths, I still find it interesting to go back and look at how their addiction was covered and compare it to the coverage of female celebrities like the late singer Amy Winehouse. I recently rewatched *Amy*, the 2015 documentary about Winehouse, and was disturbed by footage that turned her bulimia and addictions into jokes. When he announced the nominees for the best female pop vocalist at the fiftieth Grammys, comedian George Lopez read Winehouse's name and then said, "Can someone wake her up this afternoon around six and tell her?" He then referred to her as a "drunk ass" while Foo Fighters Dave Grohl and Taylor Hawkins laughed in the background. Winehouse not only had six nominations that year but also beat Foo Fighters for record of the year. Later in *Amy*, comedian Jay Leno joked that Winehouse's next album will feature "songs about cooking." The punchline: "Cooking crystal meth, black tar heroin."

Few stars became bigger punchlines for their addiction struggles than Lohan. From 2007 to 2011, she went to five different facilities and spent over 250 days in rehab. During this period, tabloids and celebrity gossip sites focused on her partying and addiction issues but rarely with any kindness or actual understanding of how addiction works. Her nights out were obsessively chronicled, with a narrative that focused on how she was wasting her talent and blowing her chances at a successful career with her late-night antics. In 2007, *Entertainment Weekly* cruelly spoofed Lohan's "best moments of 2007," which included "did not get arrested 363 days of the year" and "took second cutest mug shot of '07, trailing only Shia LaBeouf."

In 2007, paparazzi captured the widely publicized, and memed, shot of Lohan passed out in the front seat of a car. She is asleep, her mouth open and her red hair visible under a grey hoodie. The *New York Post*'s headline when it ran the photo was "SMASHED." The photo was taken Memorial Day weekend, an eventful, long one for Lohan, who, early Saturday morning, drove her Mercedes into a curb on Sunset Boulevard and received her first DUI. Later that night, she partied at the Roosevelt Hotel. She finished the weekend by entering rehab for the second of her three stays that year. Following her two 2007 DUIs, she released a statement that said: "It is clear to me that my life has become completely unmanageable because I am addicted to alcohol and drugs." In a 2014 interview with Oprah Winfrey, Lohan called herself an addict and admitted that she had used both cocaine and alcohol.

Like in the case of Spears, the reactions to Lohan's very public issues with addiction illustrated how the struggles of young women had become a spectator sport. For women like Lohan and Spears, their value and worth were no longer measured by their talent but by how far they could fall and how much of it we could witness. We delighted in tabloids and celeb gossip bloggers tearing these women apart until they were reduced to nothing but carcasses, with a few blonde hair extensions, and then we discarded them for the next young singer, actress, or former member of the cult of Disney. "In the aughts, enabled by the internet and by stigmas surrounding mental health, people reveled in the spectacle of women—particularly beautiful, famous ones—breaking down in public," wrote Sophie Gilbert in *The Atlantic*.

Seeing how Spears and Lohan were treated made me afraid to address my own issues publicly. Scared to talk about my mental health, I retreated further into myself. Even if I did reveal what I was going through, I feared it would become the thing that defined me, the thing I was always associated with, like Spears shaving her head or Lohan passed out in her car.

After the two documentaries on Spears exposed the predatory paparazzi, publications rushed to make amends. Peros, who worked at *Us Weekly* in 2007, told the *New York Times* that tabloids had since become "much more sensitive and handle stories like this more delicately." She said that mental health and addiction issues are less stigmatized now and that journalists and editors know any aggressive media coverage will trigger backlash. In February 2021, *Glamour* magazine posted an apology to Spears on their Instagram account and accepted responsibility for their part in her downfall and the coverage of it.

It's certainly true that the rise of social media has given celebrities more control and the tabloids less power. Social media can not only arm young female celebrities with the tools to tell their own stories but it can also help to call out past injustices. TikTok users showed support for Lohan after a 2013 David Letterman interview surfaced. In it, the late-night host repeatedly mocks Lohan's rehab visits and addiction issues. A visibly uncomfortable Lohan later said the rehab questions had not been raised in the pre-interview and she was caught off guard on live television. "This is so wrong on so many levels," viewers said. In a 2022 *Cosmopolitan* cover story, Lohan praised the changes social media has brought. "When I first started out in the business, none of us had a say in how to control our own narrative," she said. "There were paparazzi pictures, and then people ran with it. So I think it's really good that in this day and age, people can say who they are and who they want to be."

But it's a mistake to assume pop culture has righted its past wrongs and changed how it treats young female celebrities. Media apologies are often nothing more than lip service or a public relations strategy. They're soon forgotten, and women find their struggles again turned into spectacle. In 2021, Selena Gomez spoke out about the jeering treatment she received from the media when she revealed, and sought treatment for, her bipolar disorder. Male celebrities in similar situations are still handled with more compassion. Canadian singer Shawn Mendes recently cancelled a world tour to deal with his mental health and was applauded by the media for the decision. Pete Davidson has also been praised for being open about his mental health and for contributing to a dialogue about bipolar disorder and depression.

As for Peros's claim that magazines know better than to try any aggressive media coverage today, the truth is that misogyny sells too well to be given up. In the latest issue of *Life & Style*, Spears was on the cover: "Struggling with Freedom: Nude Selfies, Drug Binges & Breakdowns." I won't hold my breath for the backlash.

Unlikeable Women

MY FANCY CHEESE BOARD was ready, and the red wine was poured. I was celebrating the return of the Golden Globes. In 2022, NBC dropped the broadcast after an *LA Times* investigation revealed ethical lapses and a lack of diversity among voting members. The Hollywood Foreign Press Association, the organization behind the event, implemented reforms in time for the 2023 awards and hoped everyone would move on.

Glossing over the past turned out to be the theme of the night, along with Scientology jokes and white actors awkwardly shifting in their seats whenever host Jerrod Carmichael mentioned race. Brad Pitt was the evening's golden boy. He was nominated for best supporting actor for his work in *Babylon*. He didn't win, but the show's cameras, along with everyone else, loved him. Women gushed and men thanked him for being an inspiration. *Abbott Elementary* creator Quinta Brunson interrupted her acceptance speech for best musical or comedy with a "Hey, Brad Pitt." Best actor winner Austin Butler singled Pitt out with a "Brad, I love you." Later in the show, presenter Regina Hall joked the announcer got her name wrong when he failed to introduce her as "Mrs. Pitt." By the end of the night, Pitt even started to resemble a Golden Globes statue, all blonde hair and glowing skin.

Post awards, the passion for Pitt continued. *People* ran a story about his hair, "Brad Pitt Debuts New, Shorter Haircut at Golden Globes 2023." Not to be outdone in coif coverage, *Vogue* published "Brad Pitt Debuts a New Heartthrob Haircut at the Golden Globes." *E! News* called him the "life of the party," supported by a photo gallery of the actor posing with various stars. An eyewitness said, "Brad was the biggest star in the room. Everyone was trying to get face time with him."

During the ceremony, Pitt smiled, laughed, and played along. I was definitely not playing along. Midway through the ceremony, "#BradPittIsAnAbuser" started trending on Twitter, a reference to the domestic abuse allegations ex-wife actress Angelina Jolie had made against him following a 2016 flight from France to California. According to FBI records, he grabbed Jolie by the head, pushed her into a bathroom wall, punched the ceiling of the plane, poured beer on her, choked one of their children, and hit another in the face. Jolie filed for divorce five days after the incident.

Not surprisingly, Pitt denied Jolie's accusations and accused her of trying to ruin his reputation. His supporters labelled her spiteful and vindictive and called her allegations lies. *TMZ* showed whose side they were on with stories that talked about how "Jolie is on a smear campaign against Brad Pitt" and "Brad Pitt Sources Say Angelina Jolie Has Poisoned Kids Against Him." A 2017 *New York Post* piece asked, "Does Angelina Jolie really believe that anyone is buying this?" and called her a "master media manipulator."

It's worth noting that details of the 2016 allegations against Pitt were revealed only after the actor sued Jolie for breach of contract over the sale of her share in Chateau Miraval, the French winery the two co-owned. Jolie countersued, claiming the negotiations to sell her share to Pitt fell apart after he demanded she sign a non-disclosure agreement that would have prevented her from publicly speaking about his abuse of her and their children.

After the abuse allegations were made public, Pitt launched his public sympathy tour. In a 2017 *GQ* interview, he discussed sobriety and his battle with alcohol addiction. The piece was sympathetic, downplaying the abuse allegations as "a public-relations crisis" and describing the actor as "a father suddenly deprived of his kids, a husband without wife … a 53-year-old human father/former husband smack in the middle of an unraveled life, figuring out how to mend it back together." The redemption tour worked. Many social media commenters blamed Pitt's behaviour on the booze, not the man.

Pitt continued to work as an actor and producer and receive award nominations. He even produced *She Said*, a movie about Harvey Weinstein and the *New York Times* reporters who broke the story which helped the #MeToo movement gain mainstream momentum. Perhaps Pitt hoped to distract attention from his own allegations, or maybe he liked the irony of an abuser making a film about another abuser. But it seemed like an odd decision given Jolie's 2021 *Guardian* interview in which she talked about the hurt she experienced when Pitt decided to work with the Hollywood mogul despite knowing he had sexually assaulted her. (Pitt also produced 2022's *Blonde*, a fictionalized account of the life of Marilyn Monroe which fetishized her pain and suffering, so we have him to thank for that misogynistic mess.)

As Pitt rose, Jolie fell. She was repeatedly villainized, portrayed as untrustworthy and unlikeable. The unlikeable woman trope is certainly nothing new. There are the unlikeable women who supposedly ruin the male musicians they mate with—along with their bands. They range from Yoko Ono breaking up the Beatles to Nancy Spungen destroying the Sex Pistols and Lauryn Hill killing the Fugees. There are the unlikeable women vilified for their behaviour, from the vitriol Anne Hathaway faced for her perceived insincerity when accepting her 2013 best supporting actress Oscar to the criticism Constance Wu faced after she tweeted about her frustration over her show *Fresh Off the Boat* getting renewed. (She later alluded to the "sexual harassment and intimidation" she was subjected to by the show's producer.) The backlash against Wu was so severe the actress attempted suicide. Then there are the unlikeable women who refuse to conform to gendered representations of how they should act, such as Miley Cyrus, Cardi B, and Nicki Minaj. And, of course, there are the trainwrecks, the women made unlikeable by their public breakdowns: Amanda Bynes, Britney Spears, and Whitney Houston.

"In many ways, likability is a very elaborate lie, a performance, a code of conduct dictating the proper way to be," wrote Roxane Gay in a 2014 *BuzzFeed* essay. "Characters who don't follow this code become unlikable." Unlikability is a major plot point in female characters in movies and television, from *Mad Men*'s Betty Draper to Mavis Gary in *Young Adult* and Phoebe Waller-Bridge's *Fleabag*. Although these women are fictional, how they are treated, picked apart, and judged impacts how we treat the unlikeable women we see in our everyday lives, in the pages of *Vanity Fair* or on the witness stand in a high-profile celebrity trial.

Unlikeable male characters exist, of course. They are usually labelled anti-heroes. These are the Don Drapers, the Tony Sopranos, the Walter Whites. Women are never granted this outlaw status, nor are they free of judgment. We forgive, even celebrate, Draper's alcoholism, cheating, flaws, and spontaneous, selfish acts. It would have been a very different show had Draper been a woman.

Despite her fame and success, mainstream media never accepted Jolie. She won a best supporting actress Oscar for 1999's *Girl, Interrupted* and was nominated for best actress for 2008's *Changeling*. At the time, she was the highest paid actress, earning between $15 million and $20 million a film. She is also a Golden Globe and

Screen Actors Guild Award winner as well as an Emmy nominee. Jolie expanded into writing and directing with films like *In the Land of Blood and Honey* and *A Place in Time* and is recognized for her activism and humanitarian work.

But reporters prefer to focus on a different time in Jolie's life, her wild younger days. There was the drug use, the knife play during interviews, the vial of Billy Bob Thornton's blood she wore around her neck when they were married, and that time she awkwardly kissed her brother at the Oscars. She dated women, which biphobic Hollywood automatically equates with promiscuity. She wore leather pants and T-shirts on the red carpet. She was feral, she was unpredictable, she was a brunette.

Dislike for Jolie peaked in 2005, when she was blamed for Pitt's split from America's sweetheart, Jennifer Aniston. Jolie was the vixen, the trollop, the whore. Pitt and Jolie didn't officially comment on their relationship until 2006, but at that point, they really didn't need to. There had already been the July 2005 issue of *W Magazine* which featured a sixty-page photo portfolio of the two playing house, entitled "Domestic Bliss," as well as that infamous *Us Weekly* cover of Pitt, Jolie, and her son Maddox playing on a Kenyan beach. Pitt would later adopt Maddox.

"The supposed love triangle," wrote Angelica Jade Bastién in a 2022 *Vulture* piece on the cultural significance of Brangelina, "reflects an age-old dynamic that Hollywood and tabloids love to juice." From Betty and

Veronica fighting over Archie to Kelly and Brenda duking it out over bad boy Dylan on *Beverly Hills, 90210* to the countless *Bachelor*-style reality shows, we love to see ladies feuding and there's no greater prize for a woman than a man's affection.

The Brangelina backlash has always been directed at Jolie. Critics distrusted her humanitarian work, contending it was nothing more than an attempt to rehabilitate her image. It wasn't; she had been doing that work long before Mr. and Mrs. Smith fell in love. There were rumours that Pitt's friends, and most of Hollywood, hated her. She would always be the home wrecker, the wild child that couldn't be tamed. Her fate was sealed long before the first Team Aniston shirt was even printed. "After all," wrote Katie Jgln in *Noösphere*, "women can only exist in this world as one-dimensional blobs. As the Virgins or the Whores. The Good Girls or the Bad Girls. The Jennifer Anistons or the Angelina Jolies. And once you become one, that's it."

In other words, only two choices exist for women in pop culture. Once you're put in one of those boxes, it's very hard for you to escape.

Making a woman unlikeable, it turns out, isn't that hard. There's a fairly straightforward playbook to follow, and we saw it being used in the Johnny Depp and Amber Heard imbroglio of 2022.

Depp and Heard married in 2015 after meeting on the sets of the 2011 film *The Rum Diary*. Heard filed for divorce a year later and obtained a temporary restraining order against Depp, accusing him of domestic violence. Not surprisingly, Depp's lawyers said Heard was lying. The couple reached an out-of-court divorce settlement in 2016, and that appeared to be the end of the couple's legal battles and media attention.

Not quite. In 2018, Heard wrote an op-ed for the *Washington Post* titled "I spoke up against sexual violence—and faced our culture's wrath. That has to change." Heard never named Depp in the piece but referred to herself as "a public figure representing domestic abuse." When the British tabloid *The Sun* published Heard's abuse allegations, labelling him a "wife beater," Depp sued them. After Heard submitted evidence—from witnesses, emails, and photographs— that showed Depp's abuse, the judge ruled that *The Sun* had proven the article was "substantially true." In 2019, Depp tried again, this time suing Heard for defamation in a US court, seeking $50 million in damages. Depp and his lawyers argued, although Heard never named Depp in her *Washington Post* op-ed, she clearly implied that he abused her during their marriage. After her request to dismiss the case was denied, Heard countersued for $100 million. She alleged Depp had coordinated an online harassment campaign, which included petitions to get her fired from the film franchise *Aquaman* and her campaign with L'Oréal, and that Depp's then lawyer had defamed her in statements published in the *Daily Mail*.

In April 2022, the *Depp v. Heard* trial started. It was a social media sensation. *Vice News* reported: "According to data from social-media tracking firm NewsWhip, from the 4th of April to the 16th of May the Depp Heard trial amassed more social media interactions per published article than any other topic, including the Russia Ukraine war or reproductive rights." Depp was clearly the winner of all these interactions. One month after the trial began, TikTok's "JusticeForJohnnyDepp" hashtag, which featured play-by-plays of the day's court proceedings, had 11 billion views. "JohnnyDeppisinnocent" had 3 billion. The "JusticeForAmberHeard" hashtag? Forty-one million. Meanwhile, "#AmberHeardIsAPsychopath" trended on Twitter.

Instagram and TikTok memes painted Depp as the victim. Online commenters ranted about how cancel culture had gone too far and called Heard a gold digger, a vindictive liar, and an opportunist who was using the allegations and trial to raise her public profile. Reading the comments, it felt like people were watching a movie rather than following an actual trial involving real people. Depp supporters gathered outside the courtroom or tuned in to livestreams on Court TV's YouTube channel. Celebrities from Kate Moss to Sia to Javier Bardem defended Depp. "I know women who are exactly like this. They are manipulative and cold and they use their very womanhood to play victim and turn the world against the man," model and actress Ireland Baldwin wrote on Instagram.

Men's rights activists and far-right trolls capitalized on the trial, hanging on every word like Captain Jack Sparrow clinging to the mast of a pirate ship. Heard was called "a monster," "bipolar," "a crazy bitch," and "a drama queen." Her appearance and clothing were mocked. She received death threats and was referred to as "Amber Turd."

In the end, the jury found that Heard defamed Depp and acted in malice when she wrote her *Washington Post* piece. The jury awarded Depp $15 million. It also concluded that Depp, through his then lawyer, had defamed Heard and awarded her $2 million. Conservatives like Ann Coulter tweeted the verdict marked the death of #MeToo. Movement founder Tarana Burke, who started Me Too in 2006, more than a decade before the hashtag went viral, said it was impossible to kill: "The 'me too' movement isn't dead. The system is." The Me Too organization released a statement calling the trial a "toxic catastrophe."

Let's be clear: women like Heard and Jolie possess the means to fight long court battles. They can hire lawyers and public relations teams. They have resources other women dealing with abuse, divorce, and messy legal battles don't. Fame aside, the treatment of Heard and Jolie sends a strong message about how we treat survivors and women who come forward—if they're not deterred from coming forward in the first place. (In Canada, sexual assault is one of the most underreported violent crimes, with only 6 percent of incidents in 2019 being brought to the attention of police.)

In her 2022 *Vox* piece on the defamation trial, Constance Grady quoted a statement Heard made following the trial: "I'm heartbroken that the mountain of evidence still was not enough to stand up to the disproportionate power, influence, and sway of my ex-husband," she said. "I'm even more disappointed with what this verdict means for other women. It is a setback. It sets back the clock to a time when a woman who spoke up and spoke out could be publicly shamed and humiliated. It sets back the idea that violence against women is to be taken seriously."

Writing about Jolie and Heard in the *Guardian* in 2022, Arwa Mahdawi talked about how "[a]ny woman, no matter how famous, who speaks out about a powerful man is going to be treated like Amber Heard 2.0. Depp wrote a playbook men accused of misconduct seem very eager to copy." And as many women know, the playbook is certainly not restricted to famous men. I found myself living my own version of it when I was sexually assaulted by an acquaintance. After I filed a police report and publicly called him out, he launched a smear campaign and called me "a liar," "a crazy bitch," and "a psycho." Sound familiar?

Like Heard, I was repeatedly judged for not behaving like a perfect victim. People asked why I didn't immediately go to the police and why I had continued to talk to the man who assaulted me after it happened.

I was also judged for drinking before it happened. The experience was not only traumatic but also reminded me that there is still the widely held belief that sexual assault is the stranger lurking in a dark alley or someone holding a knife to your throat while they rip off your skirt.

A few months after *Depp v. Heard* wrapped, another unlikeable woman emerged. Unlike Heard and Jolie, there were no abuse accusations or high-profile court cases. Instead, this woman was scorned because of who she was dating.

Don't Worry Darling was actress Olivia Wilde's second film as director, after her 2019 critically acclaimed debut, *Booksmart*. When *Don't Worry Darling* was released, I knew very little about its plot but plenty about its behind-the-scenes drama. This drama mostly concerned Wilde's relationship with pop star and former One Direction member Harry Styles, who was starring in the film. While working on *Don't Worry Darling*, Wilde split from her fiancé and father of her two children, actor Jason Sudeikis, best known for his nine-season run on *Saturday Night Live* and his award-winning work on the feel-good comedy *Ted Lasso*. Sudeikis and Wilde met when she hosted *SNL*, and the celebrity couple were adored by the media and fans.

Wilde and Sudeikis announced their split in November 2020, and in January 2021, Wilde and Styles were photographed holding hands at a friend's wedding. It was rumoured they started dating on the sets of *Don't Worry*

Darling while Wilde and Sudeikis were still together. When her relationship with Styles became public, Wilde was called a sexual predator and faced ageist criticism for dating Styles, who is ten years younger. "I've had women judging me for separating from Jason. There are people who feel entitled to hurl horrendous insults at me and my family. Telling me I'm a terrible mother. Threatening me and my kids or saying I should lose my children," Wilde told *Vanity Fair* in October 2022.

The controversy, according to the *New York Times*, "raised questions about the film's viability and its director, Olivia Wilde." In the months leading up to the film's release, each day seemed to throw up a new piece of gossip, often implicating Wilde in a less than flattering way. There were the rumoured on-set clashes with the film's female lead, Florence Pugh, and the drama surrounding Shia LaBeouf's dismissal from the film. LaBeouf, who Styles was brought in to replace, maintained he voluntarily left the film while Wilde said he was fired. LaBeouf painted Wilde as a liar, and many were quick to use this as proof she was not to be trusted. I am not even going to mention the scandal with the salad dressing.

While Wilde's relationship with Styles made her a target on celebrity gossip sites, One Direction fan forums, and Twitter, there was one group that really wanted to take her down. An outspoken feminist, Wilde has promoted women's rights, #MeToo, and the need for women in leadership roles in Hollywood. She's participated in women's marches, supported Hillary

Clinton, and publicly criticized Jordan Peterson. This made her the perfect target for the far right, who called her a hypocrite and a fake feminist and delighted in the negative publicity she and the film received. She was called a "commie whore," "the new Queen of Crazy," and a "Hollywood harlot."

"We've observed that right-wing media, really all media, are eager for the downfall of women who are outspoken on progressive issues," Pam Vogel, Media Matters senior adviser, told *Vice*. According to a 2022 *Vice News* piece on the trolling of Wilde, progressive media watchdog Media Matters reported that, in the month leading up to *Don't Worry Darling*'s release, posts about the actress on the Facebook pages of right-wing sites like *The Daily Wire* generated the most responses. "Right-leaning pages have posted over 300 times more about Wilde, and the movie, earning over 200,000 interactions."

Not surprisingly, *The Daily Wire* also ran pro-Depp propaganda during his lawsuit against Heard. In May 2022, *Vice World News* and The Citizens, a nonprofit, reported that the outlet "spent between $35,000 and $47,000 on Facebook and Instagram ads promoting anti-Heard articles about the trial," read the piece, "eliciting some four million impressions."

Redemption can come for unlikeable women, but it often takes years. Case in point: Sinéad O'Connor. When her debut album, *The Lion and the Cobra*, was released in 1987, her record label expected to sell 25,000 copies.

Instead, it sold over 2 million. This success didn't stop O'Connor from being vilified for her androgynous style and shaved head.

The outspoken Irish singer was political, calling out racism and misogyny in the music industry and refusing to play the role of the polite female pop singer. (It emerged later that her record company had urged her to get an abortion when she got pregnant while recording the album; she refused.) When she was nominated for a 1989 Grammy, she performed at the awards with Public Enemy's logo painted on the side of her head as a show of support for artists who boycotted the Grammys over their decision not to televise the best rap performance award. O'Connor refused to have the US national anthem played at her concerts, saying she disagreed with the country's policies around censorship and the arts, but it was her infamous *SNL* appearance that ended her career.

Appearing as the musical guest in an October 1992 episode, O'Connor capped an a cappella rendition of Bob Marley's "War" by ripping a picture of Pope John Paul II in half. She urged viewers to "fight the real enemy" while flinging the torn pieces at the camera. O'Connor was protesting the sexual abuse of children by members of the Catholic Church, something John Paul II finally acknowledged nine years later.

The audience was stunned. NBC, the network that broadcast *SNL*, received over 4,000 complaint calls. The incident was front-page news, with O'Connor mocked by everyone from Madonna to Joe Pesci, who hosted the show the following week. She was later booed off the stage at a Bob Dylan tribute show. O'Connor said she had no regrets about what happened. "The media was making me out to be crazy because I wasn't acting like a pop star was supposed to act," she told the *New York Times* in 2021. "It seems to me that being a pop star is almost like being in a type of prison. You have to be a good girl."

Much of this is covered in *Nothing Compares*, a documentary exploring O'Connor's life and legacy that was released in January 2022, months after her 2021 memoir, *Rememberings*. Director Kathryn Ferguson said the timing was finally right for a documentary devoted to O'Connor. The #MeToo movement was surging in the US and elsewhere. In Ireland, same-sex marriage had recently become legal, and abortion was about to follow. "The world was on fire with women speaking out," Ferguson said in 2022. O'Connor was ostracized in the '90s for her outspokenness, but now she was an inspiration. The documentary ends with shots of Pussy Riot, Billie Eilish, and Bikini Kill's Kathleen Hanna, all trailblazers who followed O'Connor's direction.

Nothing Compares is just one example of the cultural reconsideration #MeToo inspired. Actress and activist Pamela Anderson, dismissed for decades as nothing more than a big-breasted bimbo, has been given a more sympathetic second look, as has singer Janet Jackson who, after her wardrobe malfunction during her 2004 Super Bowl half-time performance, experienced radio,

MTV, and Grammy boycotts, poor record sales, and a five-second delay added to late-night television appearances. *You're Wrong About*, the popular podcast which reconsiders people and events miscast in the public imagination, has revisited the legacies of past unlikeable women, from sexual harassment whistleblower Anita Hill to actress Anna Nicole Smith and former figure skater Tonya Harding. One of their best episodes is devoted to Monica Lewinsky, vilified and slut-shamed for her relationship with Bill Clinton. She was reduced to a beret-wearing seductress, humiliated and viciously bullied for her appearance and her weight.

In 2018, Elura Nanos, a lawyer who has written about Lewinsky and Clinton, told CBS News that the #MeToo era resulted in a shift in public perception for wronged women. And while it's great to revisit the legacies of O'Connor or Lewinsky, it's frustrating to still see *Us Weekly* writing misogynistic headlines about Britney.

Change is slow, I know. But it can also feel like pop culture Whac-A-Mole. We allow one woman her redemption arc, while another gets a Twitter takedown.

Pop Star Reinvention

For its March 2020 issue, *Vogue* commissioned three different covers of pop star Billie Eilish. In the photos, the twenty-one-year-old sported what was, at the time, her iconic hairstyle: a black shag with neon green roots. She was also dressed in her go-to outfit: baggy pants and hoodies—an oversized style that Eilish preferred then because it concealed her body and prevented her from being sexualized and judged. In his cover story, writer Rob Haskell dubbed it Eilish's "bloblike anti-fashion."

One year later, the June 2021 issue of British *Vogue* revealed a very different-looking performer. The green roots were replaced with platinum blonde soft curls. The skater-boy garb was swapped for a custom Gucci corset, Agent Provocateur lingerie, and latex gloves. It was old Hollywood glamour meets classic pin-up girl, awash in a champagne and rose palette. The cover coincided with the release of Eilish's new single, "Your Power," and her sophomore album, *Happier Than Ever*.

When the issue hit stands, it was Eilish's transformation, not her new music, that had people talking. Some loved the new look: when Eilish shared it on

Instagram, it became the fastest post to reach 1 million likes, doing so in only six minutes. But critics argued that the revealing, form-fitting lingerie betrayed the body positivity Eilish had championed, representing a beauty standard the singer had previously rallied against. The *New York Times* reported that fans felt betrayed that the singer had ditched her tracksuits, abandoning a style her fans had grown to love. (The newspaper was later criticized for using a possibly fake Twitter account as its only source.)

Eilish defended the *Vogue* cover, claiming she wasn't adopting a new style but had made an aesthetic choice specifically for that shoot. She also argued that, as a young woman, she should have the freedom to experiment with her image. "Dress how you want, act how you want, talk how you want, be how you want. That's all I've ever said," Eilish told *Vanity Fair*. "It's just being open to new things and not letting people ruin it for you."

It's not easy for pop princesses to move on. Even the term "pop princess" is a reminder of society's fetishization of youth and our desire to keep women suspended in time. Reinvention is a constant balancing act. How do you explore new facets of yourself without alienating fans? Taylor Swift summed it up best: "Live out a narrative that we find to be interesting enough to entertain us, but not so crazy that it makes us uncomfortable."

It's no surprise this can lead to an identity crisis. Eilish has spoken about the "dehumanizing" effect of fans holding on to memories of an artist—whether that be an old hair colour or an old sound. Those attachments can be especially limiting for singers who, like Eilish, got their start early and are naturally going to evolve. "The other day, I posted a video from when I had green hair, and I saw people go, 'I miss this Billie, the green-haired Billie,'" Eilish told *Elle Canada* in 2021. "I'm still the same person. I'm not just different Barbies with different heads."

This is not a new problem. Reinvention has been almost obligatory for female singers since Madonna normalized the act in the 1980s with each new album release. "They become chameleons, shedding the current version of themselves, and emerging as a shiny new thing, complete with a different look, aesthetic, and sound," Cheyenne Roundtree wrote in a *Daily Beast* piece on the gendered expectations that female pop stars—from Lady Gaga to Nicki Minaj to Ariana Grande—have had to navigate. Men may debut a new sound, but there isn't the pressure to create a whole new look to go with it. "Justin Bieber might have bleached his hair when he came out with his dance-pop album *Purpose* in 2015," wrote Roundtree, "but a dye job and a quick haircut will never amount to the lengths that female artists are expected to go to."

Nor are men punished quite as severely for their reinvention—if they are punished at all. No one knows more about this double standard than two women who ruled the aughts. In 2001, Britney Spears released her third album, *Britney*. The video for its first single, "I'm a Slave 4 U," debuted a sexier, more mature Spears. Critics were outraged by its overt sexuality, which they felt contradicted the virginity narrative Spears and the media had long promoted, and resented the singer's transition to a more dance sound from the bubble-gum pop found in her previous two albums. Gone was the girl-next-door image Spears had become famous for, replaced by G-strings and gyrating backup dancers.

The Parents Association of America urged a boycott, calling Spears a bad role model. The wife of conservative Maryland governor Bob Ehrlich said, "If I had a chance, I would shoot Britney Spears." Spears stood her ground. "I'm a 19-year-old girl about to be 20, I'm growing up and there's nothing wrong with that. Besides no matter what, I can never win, when I did '… Baby One More Time' [a single that promoted Spears as a Lolita-esque schoolgirl] they were saying I was too controversial, so you can never win," Spears told *Rolling Stone* in December 2001.

Christina Aguilera followed Spears's example. A year after Spears released "I'm a Slave 4 U," Aguilera dropped her fourth album, *Stripped*, and the single "Dirrty," which came with its own provocative video. No one threatened to shoot Aguilera, but petitions were launched to remove the video from MTV, and it was banned in Thailand. Aguilera referred to the transition as her "fuck-it moment," designed to challenge the good-girl trope she was assigned early in her career. "That was me stepping up and saying I was a woman proud of my sexuality."

Like Eilish, Aguilera and Spears maintained the sexy image makeovers were their idea. While I am all for women having agency over their sexuality and looking the way they want to look, we can't pretend these decisions are made in a vacuum—not when we have taught these young women that their worth is tied to their appearance.

In her 2020 documentary, *Miss Americana*, Taylor Swift talks about living in a society "where women in entertainment are discarded in an elephant graveyard at 35." Swift is doing everything she can to avoid that fate. Madonna is the model here. Her career longevity— it spans over four decades—is often attributed to her ability to shape-shift from *Like a Virgin*'s material girl to *Music*'s cowgirl to *Ray of Light*'s spiritual girl. Similarly, Swift knows that a fan's love is something that must be repeatedly earned, so each new album delivers a new version of her, a new era. When she released her self-titled debut album in 2006, she was a ringlet-haired teenage country singer with an acoustic guitar. The ringlets are long gone, and Swift is now a pop icon who has sold more than 200 million albums worldwide. She is the most streamed woman on Spotify and the only musical act to have five albums debut with over 1 million copies sold in the US. But there have been some bumps along the way.

Relevancy is a common reason female pop stars reinvent themselves, but changing the narrative is another, especially when public perception has shifted. Swift retreated from the public eye for more than a year following her bad blood with rapper Kanye West, which started in 2009 when Swift won best female video at the MTV Video Music Awards. Her acceptance speech was famously ambushed by West in one of the most controversial, and memed, pop culture moments. Then, in 2016, West released "Famous," which featured the lyrics "I feel like me and Taylor might still have sex / Why? I made that bitch famous," accompanied by a video that included a naked wax figure of Swift. West claimed he called Swift and received permission to reference her in the song, something Swift denied. West's then wife, Kim Kardashian, insisted that Swift was aware of the lyrics and had given her blessing. Kardashian also released video of phone conversations between the two where Swift gave her approval. Swift maintained that while she knew that she was going to be named, she was never told West was going to call her a "bitch," and indeed this word is not referenced in the video. Still, Kardashian seemed to win the argument, labelling Swift a snake. #KimExposedTaylorParty began trending on social media, with Kardashian's fans painting Swift as fake, calculating, and manipulative.

The feud with West and Kardashian wasn't the only incident that drove Swift to isolate herself. There was also intense tabloid scrutiny as well as a backlash to the references to famous exes in her songs—something male songwriters do repeatedly, without censure. Her "squad" of famous friends, which has included actress Blake Lively, model Gigi Hadid, and the Haim sisters, also came under criticism. Rather than a show of female solidarity, it was seen as yet another example of Swift's fake, self-serving white feminism and nothing more than beautiful white women flaunting their privileged lives.

People magazine quoted a source who said Swift "needed to disappear to reinvent herself. It was time to change things up and take another approach." She re-appeared in 2017 with a harder, edgier look as well as a new album, her sixth, *reputation*. Swift has always been a master at teasing with her reinventions, planting Easter eggs in videos and on social media which fans eagerly interpret. In the days leading up to *reputation*'s release, she posted cryptic teasers which included videos of a snake, widely interpreted as a reference to West and Kardashian. The album's first single, "Look What You Made Me Do," announced: "The old Taylor can't come to the phone right now. Why? Oh, 'cause she's dead."

Reputation sold over 4.5 million copies, making it the best-selling album by a female artist that year. Swift killed off her *reputation*-era doppelgänger—mere reinvention is not sufficient anymore for a female musician—and switched to pastel colours and political messages with 2019's *Lover*. In 2023, she began performing Eras, her sixth concert tour, that included 131 concerts across five continents and celebrated all of the singer's transformations.

But the celebration is also tinged with a kind of defeat. "The female artists have reinvented themselves twenty times more than the male artists," Swift has said. "They have to or else you're out of a job." Drake has transformed himself over the years, but his reinvention is respected rather than viewed as a necessity. Comparing the Drake that debuted musically in 2006 to the Drake about to release 2023's *For All the Dogs*, Bianca Betancourt wrote in *Vox*: "Both iterations of the rapper have carefully paid attention to the ebbs and flows of internet culture to craft a sound that many critics now claim will define a generation." Drake is described as "always evolving" and "a child of the internet generation who's savvily used Instagram, the press, and his lyrics to create his image." The reinvention of women like Swift is never regarded as savvy: it's seen as survival.

Pop princess rebirths have sometimes been problematic, from Madonna's geisha costume to Katy Perry's cornrows to Selena Gomez's bindi. But this kind of cultural appropriation is a symptom of a much bigger problem: the degree to which we are teaching young women that they have to constantly present new versions of themselves to succeed or to be interesting. In the words of Eilish: "Be how you want."

Female Feuds

MY JUNIOR HIGH SLEEPOVER was at a standstill. Half of the girls wanted to be Madonna, the other Cyndi Lauper. I had the deciding vote, forced to choose whether we would be wearing fingerless lace gloves and turning my friend's bed into a gondola to recreate Madonna's "Like a Virgin" video or spraying our hair bright orange and scream-singing Lauper's "Girls Just Want to Have Fun." I chose Lauper and spent the rest of the year "accidentally" left off the sleepover invite list by Team Madonna.

Lauper and Madonna's competition was front-page news during the 1980s, but in her 2012 memoir, Lauper talked about how she rarely thought about the feud—except when the press and music industry played it up. There is a long history of manufactured rivalries between women. One of the most famous featured silver-screen actresses Joan Crawford and Bette Davis, and it was fuelled by a tabloid press that loved seeing the two at each other's throats. It involved a fight over a man, failed truce attempts, and backstage battles on the sets of their 1962 film *Whatever Happened to Baby Jane?* The drama even inspired the first season of *Feud*, Ryan Murphy's award-winning series devoted to famous feuds.

In the aughts, Perez Hilton and *Us Weekly* obsessively chronicled the frenemy falling-out of Paris Hilton and Nicole Richie and feasted on the narrative of Britney Spears versus Christina Aguilera. A decade later, there was Rihanna's clash with Beyoncé. The two were rumoured to be fighting over Jay-Z, who, at the time, was both Rihanna's mentor and Beyoncé's boyfriend. The feud supposedly reignited in 2017, when Rihanna's *Anti* failed to receive a Grammy nomination for album of the year while Beyoncé's *Lemonade* did. By this point, Rihanna had had enough and took to social media to say, "I wish y'all would drop this topic and see things from the bigger picture! We don't need to be putting black women against each other!"

Pop culture's preoccupation with women at war shows no signs of abating. "There can't just be two talented women going forward and promoting their art," Tracyann Williams, a race and gender professor at New York's New School, was quoted as saying in 2018. "We buy into it. It's what sells magazines, it sells records, it sells downloads." Reality television has turned the dynamic into television gold, often with women competing for a man, the ultimate sign of a woman's worth, or with flawed female friendships at the centre of franchises like *Real Housewives*, which are premised on the idea that women are emotional, jealous, bitter, and petty.

In summer 2023, I read about the "ongoing" rift between actresses Kim Cattrall and Sarah Jessica Parker—which started when the two starred on *Sex and the City* and has been reignited by Cattrall's *And Just Like That...* cameo. Then there was singer and *American Idol* season one winner Kelly Clarkson addressing her rumoured feud with show alum Carrie Underwood, who won the fourth season. "We've run into each other a handful of times. There's no beef between us. There's nothing. We don't know each other," Clarkson said in a television interview when asked about Underwood. The media recycled the quote for days—that is, when it wasn't obsessively reporting on every detail of model Hailey Bieber duking it out with Selena Gomez, which ultimately resulted in Bieber receiving death threats from Gomez's fans.

Social media has definitely provided a new battle-ground for women. Endless TikTok dissections and Instagram comment deep dives help keep the competition and catfights going. Fans declare their allegiance with #team hashtags and obsessively analyze song lyrics and red-carpet appearances, posting clues online to support their feud theories and gossip. A recent viral video comparing Bieber's past interviews to support the fan theory that she copies Gomez reached 5 million views. The media not only provides up-to-the-minute coverage but also exhaustive explainers that rehash every bit of the history. "Here's Everything You Need To Know About Taylor Swift And Olivia Rodrigo's Rumored Feud," read a recent *BuzzFeed* headline that talked about the speculation that Rodrigo's song "Vampire" is about Swift.

Women tearing each other apart has also become an awards-show staple, right up there with complaining about the host or the length of the ceremony. Instead of focusing on who won, it's all about shade and side-eye. One of the best examples of this was the lead-up to the 2015 MTV Video Music Awards (VMAs). When Nicki Minaj's "Anaconda" was overlooked for video of the year, she took her frustration to social media, tweeting, "If your video celebrates women with very slim bodies, you will be nominated for vid of the year." Taylor Swift, whose "Bad Blood" video was nominated in the same category, took this personally. "I've done nothing but love & support you," she tweeted. "It's unlike you to pit women against each other. Maybe one of the men took your slot."

Minaj clarified she wasn't calling out Swift; Swift apologized, saying she misunderstood. It didn't matter: the media coverage was already in overdrive, and the story made headlines for weeks. Katy Perry also weighed in, tweeting, "Finding it ironic to parade the pit women against other women argument about as one unmeasurably capitalizes on the take down of a woman," a reference to Perry and Swift's long-running feud and rumours that "Bad Blood" was about Perry. Adding fuel to the fire was Perry's "Swish Swish," apparently about Swift, and Perry famously calling Swift a "Regina George in sheep's clothing," a reference to Rachel McAdams's *Mean Girls* character. The bad blood continued for years—until 2018, when Perry sent Swift an olive branch, like a literal one, on the opening night of her *reputation* tour.

If Swift-versus-Minaj wasn't your cup of tea in 2015,

there was also Miley Cyrus's showdown with Minaj. In an interview with the *New York Times*, Cyrus, who was hosting the VMAs that year, said she didn't respect Minaj's frustration about "Anaconda" not receiving a nomination, "because of the anger that came with it," and suggested Minaj was being a sore loser. When Minaj won the VMA for best hip hop video, she called out Cyrus during her acceptance speech, saying, "Back to this bitch that had a lot to say about me the other day in the press; Miley, what's good?" What's good was how much material the feud provided the press. It still comes up today.

The danger of our obsession with celebrity female feuds is not simply that it breeds competition and prioritizes gossip but that it ultimately disempowers women. "Assertive women who don't play by the rules present a threat to the order of things," wrote Anne Cohen in *Refinery29*. "[F]abricating a narrative that plays them off against each other in reductive and stereotypical roles is a way to take away that autonomy." At the 2017 American Music Awards, host actress Tracee Ellis Ross said the forty-fifth annual show would focus on "women who take up space, trailblaze and blaze trails, women with expansive and powerful voices." It was an odd theme when you consider that of the awards' twenty-eight categories, only nine included women. But it's a good thing there were so few female nominees, because it seemed they were all too busy scrapping to get on stage to accept an award. In the days that followed, *Us Weekly* attempted to reignite the supposed feud between Pink and Christina Aguilera when it asked, "Did Pink Cringe During Christina Aguilera's AMA Performance?" Social media, CNN, and *People* obliged with recaps, detailed timelines, and commentary that lasted much longer than Aguilera's actual performance. Always the voice of reason, *Vulture* tried to make peace with, "Stop Trying to Make Pink Versus Christina Aguilera Happen (Again)." It's disappointing that a show focused on celebrating women was reduced to a series of grudge matches.

If women are always foes, men always stick together. Pop culture loves celebrating the bromance, providing a perfect illustration of the gendered concept of friendship. The term "bromance" is credited to Dave Carnie, editor of skateboard magazine *Big Brother*, who coined it in the '90s to refer to the relationships that developed between male skateboarders who spent a lot of time together. Movies and television later embraced the bromance trope: from *The Hangover*, about a bachelor party gone wrong, to 2009's *I Love You, Man*, about a friendless man searching for a best man for his wedding. Countless movies honour male friendship and celebrate the buddy dynamic, from *Wayne's World*'s Wayne and Garth to *Star Trek*'s Captain Kirk and Mr. Spock. The close friendship of former president Barack Obama and vice president Joe Biden inspired countless memes in 2017, and *Succession*'s much-talked-about bromance between Tom Wambsgans and Greg Hirsch was a show highlight for many fans (not this one).

Celebrity male friendships are spared the endless frame-by-frame analysis to determine who is trashing whom. Matt Damon and Ben Affleck, for example, are praised for their enduring affection and trust. When the news broke that the two shared a bank account to support each other during their early acting days, media coverage talked about the duo's aspirational solidarity. Male friendships are treated with respect. If there are feuds, they are played for laughs. The often-funny tit for tat between Hugh Jackman and Ryan Reynolds is a recent example. If we rarely hear about men trashing other men, we also rarely see coverage of their friendships— or feuds—detract from consideration of their artistic output. "I wonder when the last time Bradley Cooper or Robert De Niro were asked in interview after interview about any argument they'd ever had," a frustrated Pink wrote on Instagram in February 2023. She was addressing her rumoured falling-out with Aguilera, which happened over two decades earlier and which kept coming up when she was promoting her new album. "We stick to the art with them, don't we?" she wrote.

If female musicians are forced to endlessly navigate media-manufactured and media-promoted feuds that obsessively cover every snub and supposed snub, it's because pop culture believes that drama is the only art women can make.

CREDITS

Earlier versions of some of these pieces were previously published in periodicals, both online and in print.

"The Problem with Middle-Aged Women": *Catapult*, 2022

"Judge a Book Not by its Gender": *Longreads*, 2021

"OCD is Not a Joke": *The Walrus*, 2021

"Jennifer Aniston Gives Birth to Teenager!": *This Magazine*, 2016 (adapted)

"Live Through This: Courtney Love at Fifty-five": *Longreads*, 2019

"The Women Who Built Grunge": *Longreads*, 2022

"Amy Deserves Better": *The Walrus*, 2023

ACKNOWLEDGEMENTS

I am thankful for the talented editors I got to work with at *Catapult*, *Longreads*, and *The Walrus*. Thank you to Tajja Isen, Peter Rubin, Lauren McKeon and Krista Stevens for your guidance and great edits. Krista, years ago you accepted a Courtney Love piece that I had given up hope on ever finding a home for. Your encouragement gave me the confidence to keep writing about pop culture and its gender bias.

Thank you to the Canada Council for the Arts for supporting my work on this book through the Explore and Create Program.

A big thank you to Carmine Starnino. Thank you for your wonderful edits, kindness, and support. Thank you to everyone at Véhicule Press: Simon Dardick, Nancy Marrelli, Jennifer Varkonyi, David Drummond. I've long been a fan of the work the press does and am so happy to be a part of it.

Thank you to my *This* family and the magazine's board of directors, editors, contributors, staff, and volunteers. There are too many of you to list here, but my time at *This* has meant so much to me and I am thankful to you all. Thank you to Julie Crysler, Judith Parker, and Joyce Byrne who were encouraging and welcoming to me during my early magazine days. Always seek out people whose names start with the letter "J" and befriend them. They will change your life.

Thank you to Graham F. Scott. I am forever grateful for the time we spent working together and am thankful we got to be not only co-workers, but also friends. There is no one I would rather explain *Jersey Shore* to. Thank you to Lauren McKeon, who I was very lucky to have as my work wife for many years. Thank you for being encouraging about my pop culture story ideas and for teaching me about writing and editing. I am so thankful for your friendship and hope we wacho together for many years to come!

Thank you to Deborah Brewster and Rebecca Gimmi for *Below Deck* texts that kept me up to date while I was writing this book. Thank you to Joanne Sincich for being the best one-person marketing department a writer could ask for.

Thank you to Sue Carter for all the pop culture chats that stretched until the wee hours of the morning and for your love, friendship, and support. Pretend that GIF of the two cats hugging is here. Joyce Byrne, many years ago you corrected a typo when I called that Broken Social Scene album *You Forgo It in People* (a better title) instead of *You Forgot It in People*. I will always be grateful that you not only caught that mistake, but have been literally and metaphorically fixing my typos ever since. Thank you for your love, friendship, and pep talks.

Thank you to my aunts and my uncle for all the love and support you have given me. Mom, thank you for your love, support, sacrifices and for being the best cheerleader a kid could ask for. I am sorry about those awful teen years.